MAN IS AN ONION
Reviews and Essays

By the same author

Poems

THE LAUGHING HYENA AND OTHER POEMS (1953)
BREAD RATHER THAN BLOSSOMS (1956)
SOME MEN ARE BROTHERS (1960)
ADDICTIONS (1962)
THE OLD ADAM (1965)
UNLAWFUL ASSEMBLY (1968)
SELECTED POEMS (1968)
THE TYPEWRITER REVOLUTION AND OTHER POEMS (1971)

Novels

ACADEMIC YEAR (1955)
HEAVEN KNOWS WHERE (1957)
INSUFFICIENT POPPY (1960)
FIGURES OF SPEECH (1965)

Non-Fiction

A COMMENTARY ON GOETHE'S *Faust* (1949)
THE WORLD OF DEW: ASPECTS OF LIVING JAPAN (1955)
THE APOTHECARY'S SHOP: ESSAYS ON LITERATURE (1957)
CONSPIRATORS AND POETS (1966)
MEMOIRS OF A MENDICANT PROFESSOR (1969)
SHAKESPEARE AND THE STUDENTS (1970)

Translations

THE POETRY OF LIVING JAPAN
(Edited with Takamichi Ninomiya, 1957)

MAN IS
AN ONION

Reviews and Essays

by

D. J. ENRIGHT

Distributed by
OPEN COURT
Publishing Co.
La Salle, Ill. 61301

800-435-6850   or   815-223-2521

First Published in the United States in 1973
by The Library Press

International Standard Book No: 0-912050-31-4
Library of Congress Catalog Card No: 72-5280

Printed in Great Britain by
T. & A. Constable Ltd, Edinburgh

CONTENTS

III

Author's Note

This heterogeneous collection of 'essays and reviews' has been divided into three hardly more homogeneous sections. The first is concerned with fiction, English, American, European and Nabokovian; the second with poetry in or translated into English; and the third with Oriental writings available in English translation, plus the unclassifiable V. S. Naipaul and that imperialist among black magicians, Aleister Crowley.

For permission to reprint I am obliged to the editors of these journals: *Encounter*, *The Listener*, *New Society*, *New Statesman*, *The New York Review of Books*, and *The Spectator*.

1

THE VIRTUE OF VERBOSITY

A Biography of Samuel Richardson

SHOULDN'T *Pamela* and *Clarissa* be basic reading for the more bookish of the Women's Lib leaders? Admittedly both novels were written by a man; and though he enjoyed more than most men the company of women, as a private citizen his ideas on the relative status of men and women were solidly conventional. But each novel deals with the defeat of a man, a man who believes that the essence of a woman lies in her maidenhead, and that taking her virginity is equivalent to triumphing over her. In each case the man is thoroughly beaten, the battle and its sequel being primarily comic in *Pamela* and wholly tragic in *Clarissa*. Mr B. gets what he wants, at the price of marrying a servant-girl, and Pamela gets what she wants—she marries upwards—at the price of marrying Mr B. Lovelace gets what he wants, at the price of drugging the girl first (surely a ruinous price for a rake as sophisticated as he is), and then finds that, far from being reduced to submissiveness, the girl is remoter from his domination than ever. Pamela marries Mr B. before seduction, Clarissa won't marry Lovelace even after. To clinch the matter, she dies: 'O the triumphant subduer! Ever above me!—And now to leave me so infinitely below her!' The best counter-stroke Lovelace can make is to die too: 'LET THIS EXPIATE!'—but it doesn't compensate.

This summary is of course reductive, especially as it refers to the novel *Clarissa*, for we take the point made by the authors of this masterly new biography[1]: '*Clarissa* is not a novel *about* seduction and sex, any more than *Antigone* is a play about burial rites'. But it is *Pamela* which stands in need of defending, not *Clarissa*. Two of Richardson's *Familiar Letters* ('Directing Not only the Requisite Style and Forms to be Observed. . .

[1] *Samuel Richardson: A Biography* by T. C. Duncan Eaves and Ben D. Kimpel.

But How to Think and Act Justly and Prudently, in the Common Concerns of Human Life') feature a servant-girl whose virtue is under attack by her master. She departs the house fairly promptly. It has been asked why Pamela, if she is so pure, doesn't do the same. Of course Pamela is special, at once a 'model' and the exception which proves the rule, but in fact she does consider quitting the battlefield:

> I had two miles and a half, and a byeway to the town; and being pretty well dressed, I might come to some harm, almost as bad as what I would run away from; and then, thought I, 'it will be reported I had stolen something, and so was forced to run away: and to carry a bad name back with me to my dear parents, would be a sad thing!'

The ideal Pamela would have gone on her way, regardless of such secondary considerations as these, thus satisfying Richardson the moralist but thwarting Richardson the novelist. The real Pamela is quite different, and many of the moral doubts readers have felt about the girl arise from our irritated sense that Richardson is doting on an ideal character who for much of the time really isn't there. For much of the time a daemon has run away with his pen and is creating a character who is sanctimonious, coy, vain, shifty, cunning, vulnerable and plucky—and inexorably present and real.

We want to see *this* Pamela win, we want to see someone so resourceful, someone who can paint Mrs Jewkes so Hogarthianly, come out on top. If coming out on top means marrying the master, we want to see her do just that. She isn't too fine for Mr B.—she will be too much for him, and that thought we relish, too. Surely what would disgust us more than Pamela's 'commercial morality'—it wasn't fun being a servant-girl in those days, least of all for a premature Scholarship Girl like her—is Goldoni's stage version, which made her the daughter of a lord in disguise and thus fit to marry a gentleman. It is pleasing to hear from Messrs Eaves and Kimpel that later on a French adaptation of Goldoni fell foul of the Committee of Public Safety, who restored Pamela to her original status as a servant and a girl of the people.

Turning to Clarissa, our first question will be, Did he who made Pamela make thee? He did, whoever he was—he who created that splendid comic character also created this great tragic character, it is the same daemonic possession at work, Clarissa runs away with the mild-mannered middle-class printer just as Pamela has done... And so do other characters, notably Lovelace, for this is an altogether richer composition. Like the earlier part of *Pamela*, *Clarissa* is monstrously flawed, yet solid enough to bear flaws without cracking, enormously long, yet seemingly unamenable to abridgement: a friend who essayed to abridge the first seven letters had to admit failure: 'You have formed a style... where verbosity becomes a virtue'.

Something similar could be said of this biography, except that the flaw is none of the authors' responsibility since it resides in the irremediable fact that Richardson's outward life was abnormally uneventful. Even then, as they point out in mock self-extenuation:

> For anyone interested in literature, the apparently complete divorce between the author of *Clarissa* and the kindly but slightly ridiculous printer who collected the *Moral and Instructive Sentiments* makes Richardson an especially good example of the creative mind at work, unsupported by learning, analytic intelligence, or even much experience, and thus thrown back on its own native strength.

The lengthy sections on Richardson's friends and on his printing business are rich in historical interest but rather too detailed for the lay reader: there is a point at which the exhaustive becomes the exhausting. Yet in skipping the reader risks losing much of eminently human interest. To have had and held such friends Richardson couldn't have been merely the oily, complacent, narrow- and dirty-minded person as which he has been represented, and which at times he still seems. Such lively and diverse friends as Mrs Laetitia Pilkington, also friend of Colley Cibber and perhaps too many other men, who none the less showed a lively concern for Clarissa; and Lady Bradshaigh, a wholly respectable married woman and something of a Lady Bountiful, who formed a fondness for Lovelace which alarmed Richardson and sought to persuade him to arrange a marriage between his two characters: 'Now make Lovelace and Clarissa unhappy if you dare'.

When Richardson insisted on rape, Lady Bradshaigh pleaded that Lovelace should fall into a fever, Clarissa agree to visit him on his deathbed and out of compassion promise marriage, whereupon Lovelace should recover—and after a decent interval Clarissa would carry out her promise. Richardson, who in any case was bent on writing a Religious Novel to do with the awful but universal subject of Death and not a trite story of the Reformation of a Rake, maintained that a reformed Lovelace ought to marry not Clarissa but one of the girls he had seduced earlier. Though in practice a benefactor of Magdalens, Lady Bradshaigh rejected this view because of her low opinion of those 'who are so weak as to be tempted by such an old bait as a promise of marriage'. Rightly or wrongly, Richardson was right, but we have to admire the vivacity of Lady Bradshaigh's contentions. Her liking for Lovelace was not entirely illegitimate: 'the light, quick, sharp style of Lovelace, with its wit and its extravagance of fancy, entirely unlike anything one would have expected from Richardson,' say Messrs Eaves and Kimpel, 'is in our opinion his great triumph in writing'. And the Marquis de Sade's sickly approval of the unhappy ending (and the delicious tears caused by the spectacle of virtue crushed by vice) is almost enough to make us wish for a happy one. Despite the occasional excess of fervour, we must ask ourselves how many later novelists have engaged in such warm, prolonged and often intelligent debates with their readers. These days only writers of radio and TV serials are reproached for killing off or mismarrying their characters.

This book is also impressive in its literary criticism, firm, unindulgent, reasoned and subtly appreciative. The authors' strength is indicated in these sentences:

Readers who find abstract statements about social relationships or illustrations of the doctrines of psychoanalysis of primary interest may read *Clarissa* in the light of one of these myths or, if they are clever enough, make up their own. We will discuss the novel, as Richardson's simple contemporaries (including Diderot and Johnson) read it, in terms of its realistic surface, of its characters and of the emotions they feel and inspire and the attitudes they embody and convey.

Their witty asides, though unobtrusive, are aptly placed to spur the reader on his long journey. Apropos of Pamela's desire to be treated as a person and not as a thing, they write, 'One cannot but sympathise with her demand: even today, a young girl who does not want to be raped ought not to be raped.' On the subject of sexual symbolism they suggest that the 'very large number of longish-shaped objects used in everyday life' makes it extremely hard to avoid, 'unless one has been warned by reading Freud'. And of 'boldness' in realism, they remark that it is 'a popular word today in jacket blurbs, though a rather strange one at a time when a writer risks nothing'. All in all, it is difficult to imagine a biography of Richardson more definitive than this one, let alone more readable. (1971)

THE MAN WITHIN

The Memoirs of Graham Greene

AGAIN and again in these memoirs[1] occurs an incident or a reflection which belongs unmistakably to the world of Graham Greene's novels. 'I have tried, however unsuccessfully, to live again the follies and sentimentalities and exaggerations of the distant time, and to feel them, as I felt them then, without irony.' Then the child was indeed father of the novelist. Or is it that the mature man, his character formed, sees in his own past his own present—and sees, if he is a novelist, another characteristic novel? Does the autobiographer impose on his past his later vision of life, or does that later vision grow out of early insights and blindnesses incurred? Perhaps in most cases, probably in this case, it is a mixture of the two. Memory is selective, and the writer then selects from memory, and thus imposes on parts of the past parts of the present which have grown out of it. What a man is shapes what he writes, and what he writes shapes what he is. We confirm ourselves by living, and perhaps we confirm ourselves even more by writing: sometimes we make caricatures of ourselves.

However, there is no evidence of caricature of self or of others in this book. On the contrary, Greene works with a light touch, moving on quickly, reflecting as he must, but reflecting briefly and moralising very little, as if consciously resisting the temptation to take novelistic liberties with lives and souls created by some greater author. There are no Greene characters here, heroes or villains, but there are plenty of hints of them, plenty of evidence of a man who knew enough of their ways to create them—and sometimes, as has happened, to over-create them.

'The first thing I remember is sitting in a pram at the top of a hill with a dead dog lying at my feet.' Then memories of a canal where people were always drowning themselves or being

[1] *A Sort of Life* by Graham Greene.

drowned. Of an uncle who died at 93: 'the first sign of his approaching end was when my old aunts while undressing him removed a toe with his socks'; and a sister who fell off a mountain and got married to the man who photographed her fall: 'perhaps she admired his presence of mind'. At 16 he sat on a gravestone with Peter Quennell 'and we both read aloud to each other from *The Yellow Book* with a sense of daring and decadence'. Reading much more influential—or congenial— was provided by Browning, some of whose lines, he says, 'have influenced my life more than any of the Beatitudes', and he suggests these lines as an epigraph for all his novels:

> Our interest's on the dangerous edge of things.
> The honest thief, the tender murderer,
> The superstitious atheist, demi-rep
> That loves and saves her soul in new French books . . .

At an early age he came to know in his heart that 'I belonged on the side of the victims, not of the torturers', and this recognition ensured that his schooldays should be rather more than usually wretched. He had entered 'a country in which I was a foreigner and a suspect, quite literally a hunted creature, known to have dubious associates'. For he was the son of the headmaster and the younger brother of the head of the house. Surrounded by the forces of the resistance, as he puts it, he couldn't join them without betraying his family. Greeneland is a colony of England, or of English boarding schools: 'The sneering nicknames were inserted like splinters under the nails'. The sequel to a story of bullying and betrayal and Greene's long-nursed desire for revenge unfolds in Kuala Lumpur 33 years later, when the victim met his tormentor in the Cold Storage shop during the Christmas rush. A foxy-faced man with a small moustache, attached to Customs and Excise and keen on polo, who reminisced, 'What inseparables we were. . .' This is where Greeneland borders on Maughamland.

School was so bad that Graham eventually ran away. His head full of Henty, Stevenson and Buchan, he took to Berkhamsted Common, where he was soon captured by his sister. The outcome was a course of psychoanalysis, an astonishing

B

thing (as he remarks) for a boy of 16 in 1920. The Common was Greene's battlefield, and here as an undergraduate he fought deadly boredom by playing Russian roulette with his elder brother's revolver. In all he tempted death six times— 'the chance, of course, was five to one in favour of life'—and then stopped. Convinced, perhaps, that he was meant to go on living, and to find out that for so many writers the only respectable and handy defence against boredom is to write.

After a holiday interlude as a young gentleman-spy *à la* Buchan in the Ruhr in 1924, and much uncertainty as to his career in more mundane spheres, Greene joined *The Times* as a sub-editor and set up as a novelist. Suspected epilepsy posed a spiritual problem briefly, since, now a Catholic, he was intending to marry, but the diagnosis was found incorrect. Author of a successful first novel (*The Man Within*, 1929), he left *The Times*, and wrote two unsuccessful novels. The present book ends there, with failure. 'If there are recurrent themes in my novels it is perhaps only because there have been recurrent themes in my life. Failure seemed then to be one of them.'

A Sort of Life is not an overtly personal work but rather an account of the growth of a writer. There exists a curious and displeasing notion that only through 'confession', total frontal self-exposure, can a true and honest autobiography be written. But nothing is more untrustworthy than deliberate introspection in public. 'There is a splinter of ice in the heart of a writer,' says Greene—and the ice tends to melt too readily when the writer is engaged upon his own heart. A man is best revealed when he works, and in his comments on his work and its context, or on his family and his friends and enemies. The best recent autobiography is to be found in books like Harold Owen's *Journey from Obscurity* and V. S. Pritchett's *A Cab at the Door*, where the authors are ostensibly writing about something other than themselves, something which enables them to reveal themselves obliquely—and decently and tellingly. By their fruits we shall know men, not by their tendentious self-guided self-tours.

Greene says that, perhaps because of his admiration for the Metaphysical poets, he was given to exaggerated similes in his early writing, and his wife became adept at shooting down these 'leopards'—so called after a particular example 'comparing something or someone in the quiet landscape of Sussex to a leopard crouching in a tree'. He adds that 'it took a great many years for me to get the beasts under control, and they growl at me sometimes yet'. Yes, we think of 'He drank the brandy down like damnation' and 'Heat stood in the room like an enemy'. They still growl occasionally ('The sneering nicknames were inserted like splinters under the nails'), and this book helps to explain them. And also to remind us that there are less attractive beasts than leopards, and that in the jungle of contemporary writing—or, rather, the barnyard—Graham Greene stands out as a decent and humane figure. (1971)

ART SHARES ITS BREAD

On Malcolm Lowry

FOR the exegetes the prize item in this selection of Malcolm Lowry's letters will certainly be the defence of *Under the Volcano* which Lowry submitted to Jonathan Cape in early 1946.[1] Considering the perils which beset an author engaged in defending his work against a publisher's reader, the letter is indeed impressive: the tone is impeccable, cheerfulness is always breaking in, and Mr Cape's only objection could have been (again) to Lowry's length. The curious aspect of this interchange is that we see the justice both of the reader's criticisms and of Lowry's replies. The novel is too long, the beginning is slow (and alas one needs to re-read it after reaching the end), the character drawing is weak. And yet, in practice, these defects don't matter to the extent that they ought in theory. The slowness of the beginning is the slowness of convalescence and reminiscence, the lengthiness is the lengthiness of what the Consul called 'the longest day in his entire experience, a lifetime', and as for the weakness of the character drawing, perhaps we can admit that Lowry was right: 'there just isn't *room*: the characters will have to wait for another book . . .' Or we can agree that, at any rate, the other characters or non-characters don't really matter, what really matters is the Consul, and if he isn't a character, then characters are not indispensable to major works of arts.

One is touched to see what a blow Lowry felt the prior publication of *The Lost Weekend* to be. This he considered 'an excellent study'—and could there be room for two studies of dipsomania?—but he suggested to Cape that perhaps '*Volcano* was, so to say, a couple of turns of the screw on *The Lost Weekend*'. In order to demonstrate the nature of these turns he went on to explain its symbolism, an aspect in which that other

[1] *Selected Letters of Malcolm Lowry*, edited by Harvey Brett and Margerie Bonner Lowry.

novel was certainly not a competitor. Thus Mexico 'is the
world itself, or the Garden of Eden, or both at once'. The
omnipresent movie, *Las Manos de Orlac*, refers us to the guilt of
mankind. The Ferris wheel is Buddha's wheel of the law, and
other things besides. Hugh is 'Everyman tightened up a screw',
and the same person as the Consul. The Consul's drunkenness
symbolises 'the universal drunkenness of mankind during the
war, or during the period immediately preceding it', and the
volcanoes are 'a symbol of approaching war'. Yvonne is 'the
eternal woman . . . angel and destroyer both'; and when she
imagines herself gathered up into the stars whereas the Consul
is flung into the abyss, this is a parallel with Marguerite (carried
up to heaven) and Faust (dragged down into hell). Not to
mention the cabbalistic significances, the Dantesque parallels,
the political allegory . . .

Although Lowry explicates his work with as much grace as
can be granted that ambiguous undertaking, indeed not merely
inoffensively but endearingly, this document is likely to repel
anyone who has not yet read *Under the Volcano*—unless of
course he is totally addicted to the symbolical, or intending to
take an examination in the book. The reaction of those who
already know the novel will probably be of this kind: 'Yes, I
supposed he was getting at something of that sort, but it didn't
seem to matter then'. And it doesn't really matter now. If we
are concerned for the fate of Faust it is because Faust is a man—
and if we are concerned for the fate of the Consul it is not
because he 'is' Faust but because he too is a man. 'The esoteric
business was only a deep-laid anchor anyway.' One splendid
thing about Lowry's apologia is his insistence that the 'symbols'
in the novel are legitimate not because they are symbols but
because they are real. The madman who is briefly seen throwing a tyre in front of him, picking it up and throwing it again:
this is a symbol of futility, but it and the other symbols and
projections of states of mind 'are *right*, are *true*, are what one
sees here'. Death under the hooves of a runaway horse in a
thunderstorm 'is nothing like so unusual an occurrence as
you might suppose in these parts, where the paths in the
forests are narrow . . .' The vultures are 'more than cartoon
birds: they are real in these parts, in fact one is looking at

me as I write, none too pleasantly either'. And the volcanoes too are real volcanoes, and pariah dogs actually exist in Mexico . . .

In a state of drunkenness 'rare with him', the Consul finds himself on an empty but active looping-the-loop machine, sitting in what seemed like a little confession box. Hardly a dignified position for an ex-representative of His Majesty's Government, he reflects, 'though it was symbolic, of what he could not conceive, but it was undoubtedly symbolic'. It was symbolic of life, of a possible part of a possible life. And Lowry would have concurred with William Faulkner's reply to Malcolm Cowley's query about the symbolic implications in his work:

Art is simpler than people think because there is so little to write about. All the moving things are eternal in man's history and have been written before, and if a man writes hard enough, sincerely enough, humbly enough, and with the unalterable determination never quite to be satisfied with it, he will repeat them, because art like poverty takes care of its own, shares its bread.[1]

In his foreword to a new edition of Under the Volcano, Stephen Spender remarks that the symbols and myth-elements illustrate the story and help to reveal the characters, whereas in Eliot and Joyce (at any rate Finnegans Wake), those 'school-masters of poetry' whom Lowry so much looked up to, the story and the characters are there for the sake of the myth, the particular exists for the sake of the universal. The Consul may be 'a symbol of mankind', but what we are given is a man's-eye view of him, not a god's-eye view. The composition of Under the Volcano was no escape from personality: Lowry was writing about himself, not about 'civilization' or 'the mind of Europe'; he was a humanist, not a symbolist; far from standing au-dessus de la mêlée, he was in the very midst of it. He is, Spender proposes, a romantic: certainly he is remote from the classical schoolmasters! And we do ourselves and the novel no service by seeking to translate it into those large con-

[1] See The Faulkner-Cowley File by Malcolm Cowley.

siderations towards which *The Waste Land*, *Finnegans Wake* and the *Cantos* point the reader with a distinctly more imperious hand.

One does not have to be a publisher's reader to perceive the weaknesses in *Under the Volcano* or in Lowry's other books. The writing is not infrequently amateurish, in a do-it-yourself way; in spots it is even embarrassingly simplistic and sentimental. Yvonne's letters are novelettish; the Consul wonders whether she has been reading the letters of Heloise and Abelard: she 'had certainly been reading *something*'. And sometimes we suspect Lowry had been reading something too. Thus Hugh's first sight of Yvonne in Chapter IV: 'and then his heart and the world stopped too . . .'. In fact neither of them stopped. Thus such declamations (albeit generally brief) as 'What was life but a warfare and a stranger's sojourn?', which is followed however by a magnificent description of riding on horseback downhill and through a river; or 'Christ Jesus why may we not be simple, why may we not all be brothers?', which can perhaps be condoned, as a simple and heartfelt desideration, in a novel which cogently and reluctantly illustrates our inability to be simple and exemplifies the obstacles which stand in the way of our all being brothers.

A graver criticism is that in a work where so much is explained, so much of importance still goes unexplained. (It takes the letter to Cape to assure us that Yvonne *is* killed by the horse!) There is a softness, a cloudiness, a sentimentality, at the heart of the novel. What is wrong with the Consul, why is he drinking himself to death? The explanation doesn't lie in his wife's infidelity, however powerfully (the more so because so succinctly) the hurt of jealousy is conveyed: for that, as he knows, would never have occurred but for his drinking, but for his rejection of love in favour of mescal. Yet to complain of this absence of motivation is hardly more damaging than to object to the suddenness and irrationality of Leontes' jealousy in *The Winter's Tale*. Undeniably the Consul is perverse, lazy, selfish and self-pitying. He knows it, he recognises 'his own fruitless selfish ruin', and he goes to his end like a man, even almost like a gentleman, certainly like a wit and a dandy. 'The Consul's despair,' Spender writes, 'is really acedia,' and we may think of

Hamlet, another character whose emotions have been held to lack an 'objective correlative'. Acedia, in that case, is a remarkably lively state of being! Whatever the reasons for the Consul's degeneration, that degeneration itself is presented in such material detail and with such fantastic vigour and absorptive power that the reader, or some readers at least, cannot help but respond, 'There, but for the grace of . . .'. In part this power derives from Lowry's humour, a quality which manifests itself throughout the letters and particularly in the grimmer contexts, as part and parcel of his vitality and courage and even hopefulness. 'Delowryum tremens' indeed!

Writing of *Under the Volcano*, Lowry was at pains to point out that 'I meant parts of it to be funny, though no one seems to have realised that'. He instanced the Taskerson episode, which is, fairly plainly, funny and (as Spender says) 'joyous and outgoing'. Humour is obvious enough, one would have thought, when the Consul, having turned on the water in the basin, finds himself standing under the shower, 'waiting in an agony for the shock of cold water that never came'. More commonly the wit is what is called verbal. Thus, at a bad moment, with his neighbour Mr Quincey's words knocking on his consciousness:

Old De Quincey; the knocking on the gate in Macbeth. Knock knock: who's there? Cat. Cat who? Catastrophe. Catastrophe what? Catastrophysicist. What, is it you, my little popocat? Just wait an eternity till Jacques and I have finished murdering sleep! Katabasis to cat abysses. Cathartes atratus . . .

The novel is more than what is called 'nightmarish', because the Consul stays awake throughout, sometimes crudely awake, as in his reaction to the pimp's reply in being asked the time: 'half past sick by the cock'. The humour is generally more subtle (though in a book of this nature one doesn't want only subtlety): at another bad moment, 'a procession of thoughts like little elderly animals filed through the Consul's mind'. Probably the best example is the mangled epitaph of Dr Vigil. 'Poor your friend, he spend his money on earth in such continuous tragedies.' The Consul's downfall does not assert or imply change and decay in all around. *Under the Volcano*, with something of a comparable hypnotic potency, possesses something of that paradoxical motion which Leavis noted in Keats's *Ode to a Nightingale*: 'we find that it moves outwards and upwards towards life as strongly as it moves downwards towards extinction'.

Now that he is safely dead, Lowry's star is in the ascendant. Alas, to judge by a hectic post-mortem by the equally late Conrad Knickerbocker in the *Paris Review* for Summer 1966, he is becoming a literary legend in the great tradition of Dylan Thomas and Brendan Behan. That cannot be helped: he did not have the fastidiousness or the forethought of William Faulkner. And perhaps his slow and comparatively recent rise to fame is also explicable. Readers who have come to question the grandiose significances of the modernists, the great schoolmasters of literature, have naturally come to welcome (a strange way of putting it, even so!) a novel which portrays, not the decline of 'civilisation' (we have perceived that there are *several* civilisations, and not all but one of them are to be aptly defined as 'hooded hordes'), but the decline and death of one man. A man who might—as the Fisher King never could—be us. (1967)

SHIVERY GAMES

Doris Lessing's 'Children of Violence'

THE FOUR-GATED CITY is the fifth and last (irrevocably the last) of the novels which make up Doris Lessing's sequence, 'Children of Violence', and in the most obvious sort of way it does more than its predecessors to account for the over-all title. Otherwise, and apart from the continuing technique of total evocation, it would hardly seem to come from the same pen.

In the first four novels Mrs Lessing is a conscientiously realistic writer, dealing with many (if not all!) of the political and social issues which have engaged the international intelligentsia since the end of the First World War. Personally I find the writing in these books somewhat undistinguished, artisan rather than artistic—in the present book, why use a word like 'matriarchical', why perpetrate a sentence like 'She comforted Lynda that she was not to worry, Algavious (she called him Al for short) would take off her, Lynda, with her, Sandra, when it was time'?—and the detail of the narration impresses me as quite suffocating at times. Mrs Lessing has never trusted to the illuminating image or the revealing instance, the part which could evoke the whole more accurately than the whole can ever do: she spells everything out. At the same time, except for that quasi-mystical communion of the flesh, so very, very conscious, which comes early in the present novel, her spelling is good and careful; she takes pains with her documentation; she adopts attitudes and sides, and they are always decent ones. She knows what is right, what is good, but she doesn't make either the ends or the means seem simpler than they are, and like a true liberal she inclines to say more for the bad attitudes and the wrong sides than they would bother to say for themselves. Her *roman fleuve* moves sluggishly—Martha Quest's prime seems to last for a good fifty years!—but it has a certain grim carrying power about it.

If Mrs Lessing is more concerned with matter than with style, then at least this is preferable to the contrary state of affairs. Her work is free of gimmicks, a fact which endows it with distinction at a time when so many novels turn out to be gimmicks *et praeterea nihil*. To take but a few recent examples: an old-fashioned country boy's adventure retold in four-letter words; a faded novelette of stock situations injected with modish voyeurism; a thin and oft-told tale lacquered over with such painstaking obscurity as to suggest profound originality to over-worked reviewers and under-developed readers . . . All about as inventive as the Black Mass. No, Mrs Lessing works for her royalties: she is a stakhanovite of contemporary fiction.

Yet this new and final instalment does decline, I fear, into reliance on a gimmick—the gimmick of the apocalyptic, or the science-fictional, which here takes the form of a not very specific 'Catastrophe' resulting from the escape of nerve-gas from a research station and/or accidents involving nuclear devices. Unhappily there is no true—no artistically true— connection between the Martha Quest whom we first met as a 15-year-old in the novel named after her and the old woman whose death on a contaminated island somewhere off Scotland is casually mentioned in the 'Appendix' to *The Four-Gated City*. While we recognise that our own lives could end in this way, our own 'quest' be terminated by an atomic holocaust willed or accidental, we may still feel resentment when this is made to happen to fictitious characters in a work of fiction. There is nothing intrinsically impossible or even improbable in Mrs Lessing's 'Catastrophe', a real Martha Quest could certainly end this way—but it won't do for Mrs Lessing's Martha. Moreover, it is not merely that *The Four-Gated City* doesn't consort with the earlier four books: the greater part of this fifth book, which is itself densely documentary and indeed rather tediously domestic in its detail (every breakfast egg-and-bacon is fried in print), doesn't consort with its own ending.

We cannot deny Mrs Lessing her vision of disaster, her despair. The world can quite conceivably meet the fate she describes. The trouble, as I have suggested, is that this fate is not in accordance with the rest of 'Children of Violence', and neither is it effectively, with an effect of significant irony, out of accord with it. It may be the case that the long stretches describing the mental breakdowns of a number of characters are intended to act as a bridge between the domestic and the apocalyptic, the collapse of the individual preparing us for the collapse of society. One reason why this doesn't work out is that the breakdowns are repetitious and boring to read about, quite as boring as detailed descriptions of people's appendectomies—and at least in the latter case no character could have more than one to be described! Communism has quite lost its appeal, independent Africa has proved a sad disappointment and especially to its best friends—we form the impression that, having run out of good causes, Mrs Lessing has turned petulant and decided to punish the intelligentsia either by killing them off or (worse) making them look very silly.

The effect is somewhat as if C. P. Snow's series, 'Strangers and Brothers', were to be taken over towards its close by the author of *Giles Goat-Boy*. Or, since Mrs Lessing describes 'Children of Violence' as 'what the Germans call a *Bildungsroman*' (in which case we shall ask the more aggrievedly, 'Was it for this the clay grew tall?'), as if *Wilhelm Meister's Apprenticeship* were to have the concluding pages of Günter Grass's *Dog Years* tacked on to it. Yet, broken-backed as it is, *The Four-Gated City* is still largely readable by virtue of its rewarding incidentals. Mrs Lessing's indignation about mental hospitals and the treatment of the mentally disturbed—this we can admire, though later we may ask, But why get so worked up about mental hospitals when you are about to reduce a sizable part of the world to chaos? Better psychiatric methods could hardly have saved Mrs Lessing's people, for it was the 'sane', not the 'sick', who were busily making the nerve gases and the nuclear devices.

The reactions of a newly arrived colonial to England are excellently depicted. To ascertain the unwritten laws of social intercourse, to determine when and where you may rightly grumble and when and where you mustn't, to know when to anticipate hostility from the natives and when friendliness—these tricky problems confront even British-born expatriates who 'go home' briefly every other year or so. The visit to London of Martha's mother, an old lady from 'white' Africa, is very well done, exquisitely painful to share in. And the account of the 1950's and 1960's with scholarship boys storming out of the provinces and the Aldermaston marches, is good too, though this fictional Life-and-Thought could have been improved by the presence of a few more sharply realised exemplars. Mrs Lessing has some sound remarks about the shadow-boxing of the British press and other mass media:

> Apparently it was a scene of debate, competition, violently clashing interests . . . The newspapers that remained might call themselves right, left or liberal, but the people who wrote for them were interchangeable, for these people wrote for them all at the same time, or in rapid succession. The same was true of television: the programmes had on them the labels of different companies, or institutions, but could not be told apart, for the same people organised and produced and wrote and acted in them. The same was true of the theatre. It was true of everything.

Including the literary columns: either you get reviewed by the whole metropolitan press or you get reviewed by none of it. For all the show of rivalry and independence of judgement, etc., it's as if the editors have gone into a huddle to decide which new books to notice and also how to notice them. That Mrs Lessing is so shrewd about things as they are makes one resent the more sharply her uneasy excursion into Things to Come.

It could be argued that she has prepared us for 'the Destruction' by hints conveyed in the epigraphs to Part One of *Martha Quest*—'I am so tired of it, and also tired of the future before it comes' (Olive Schreiner)—and to Part Three of *Landlocked*—'My God, in what a century you have caused me to live!' (St Polycarp)—and we have failed to take them seriously enough. Also that what we had supposed to be a representatively reactionary pronouncement by Mr Maynard in *A Ripple from the Storm*, the third novel in the series, is in fact a reasonably accurate description of the state of the world just before 'the Catastrophe':

> What is history? A record of misery, brutality, and stupidity. That's all. That's all it ever will be. What does it matter who runs

a country? It's always a bunch of knaves administering a pack of fools.

In a similar spirit it could be held that a further link resides in the 15-year-old Martha's day-dream of 'the golden city' with four gates, the 'noble city, set foursquare and colonnaded along its falling flower-bordered terraces', which recurs in the novel called *A City in the Desert* written by Mark Coldridge within the novel *The Four-Gated City*, but emphatically does not occur in the real world. Yet not to expect Utopia isn't the same as anticipating Armageddon . . . It is difficult to believe that the author of *Martha Quest* really intended the sequence to end as it does. Even so, we ought to give that ending a closer look.

Writers of science fiction generally contrive to leave the door open for the resuscitation of our species, or for the emergence of a better one, closing their apocalyptic chronicles with something along the lines of Zeitblom's 'high G of a cello', in Thomas Mann's *Doctor Faustus*, his 'light in the night'. In *The Four-Gated City*, it appears that the women busily having those tedious breakdowns were in truth developing extrasensory powers: they knew that a disaster was on its way, though they couldn't tell what or when. Intellectuals still, they debate in cheering fashion the effects of telepathy on government—no more secret treaties, no more secret research, no more thought-control, how could authoritarianism survive? But 'the Catastrophe' happens. Later on, among the children born to survivors in Martha's group, there are several 'listeners' and 'seers', in the manner of John Wyndham's story, *The Chrysalids*, who 'carry with them a gentle strong authority', and tell their elders that 'more like them are being born now in hidden places in the world, and one day all the human race will be like them . . .' But when one of them, the 'marvellous child' Joseph, is sent by Martha to a 'Reconstitution and Rehabilitation Centre' in Nairobi, he is at once classed as 'subnormal to the 7th, and unfit for academic education'. This could be ascribed to the last-ditch stupidity and fearfulness of the old world, of course, but no firm reassurance is forthcoming, and alas some of the 'new people' are said to have two heads and fifty fingers, which doesn't sound like the beginnings of any very brave new world. Right at the end, 'And what next?' asks Mark Coldridge, the novelist within the novel, now an old man. 'Oh how full the world is now of brotherly love and concern! . . . If one hundredth of all this love and money had been spent *before* to teach something as simple as that if you light a fuse a bomb will go off, then . . . We are all brothers now, except for these who might turn out not to be . . .' If only, if only—we end with the vain lament of a defeated liberal.

'Things are grim enough without these shivery games. People frightening one another—a poor sort of moral exercise . . .' Saul Bellow's Herzog had some sensible and timely things to say about this modern and modish business. 'We love apocalypses too much, and crisis ethics and florid extremism with its thrilling language. Excuse me, no. I've had all the monstrosity I want.' I think *The Four-Gated City* is open to this rebuke. Finally, however, it may well be that most readers will object less to the apocalyptic end than to the tedious means whereby it is arrived at, the gratuitous lengthiness of the work. It only took God six days to create the whole world. It really shouldn't require six hundred pages for Mrs Lessing to destroy a part of it. (1969)

PUBLIC DOCTRINE AND PRIVATE JUDGING

Muriel Spark

PERHAPS because I first read Muriel Spark merely for the sake of reading, perhaps because I read her books in odd foreign parts where they had been untimely ripped from their dust-covers and hence bore no biographical data, I did not realise that she was a Catholic novelist. The one thing that everybody knew about this author lay unknown to me. But this deficiency is now supplied, and I can see that the novels could be held to bear out the dust-cover's directions: they have Catholics in them, and a good deal of reference to Catholic doctrine. Indeed, *The Mandelbaum Gate* would suggest quite strongly, by its detailed and sometimes 'loving' descriptions of the Holy Land, that its author could well be a practising Christian, or else a practising archaeologist, or (though less likely) a botanist with a particular interest in wild-flower seed-dispersion. And its characters might seem to indicate that their author is a Christian, or else a Moslem, an Israeli, or an Arab, a diplomat, or a spy—or even, come to that, possibly a novelist.

Not that I wish to take Mrs Spark's faith—that 'beautiful and dangerous gift'—away from her. On the contrary. But there is a difference between a Catholic who writes novels and a Catholic Novelist. This latter term evokes, even if it shouldn't, an unholy mixture of the Claudelic, the Mauriacesque and the Greenean, a browbeating either direct or indirect, a stifling odour of incense or of fallen sweat or of both. Mrs Spark's writing seems to me altogether dissimilar: even a lapsed Wesleyan can approach her without too painful a sense of intimidation or exclusion. Yet most discussion in print of Mrs Spark's work centres on her Catholicism—and rarely gets far away from it. In an otherwise subtle article appearing in the

New Statesman on the publication of *The Girls of Slender Means*,
Frank Kermode described her as 'an unremittingly Catholic
novelist'—unremitting? Mrs Spark?—while Granville Hicks
has faintly deplored her as 'a gloomy Catholic, like Graham
Greene and Flannery O'Connor, more concerned with the
evil of man than with the goodness of God'. Far from gloomy,
I would even have thought her positively funny, and—though
admittedly this new novel lends one more conviction on this
point than might otherwise have been felt—concerned with
the evil of man no more than is to be expected in a fairminded though shrewd observer of humanity.

Yet there may be some truth in the negative aspect of Mr
Hicks's complaint, for Mrs Spark the novelist does at times
seem a mite sceptical about the goodness of God, or (which to
some people will be the same thing) about the power and
efficacy of God's goodness. The ways in which God moves are
occasionally too mysterious for 'goodness' to seem the immediately, the patently and indisputably *mot juste*. The horrors
in her novels are not fortuitous, and they are too ingenious to
be other than supernatural or preternatural in origin. The
horror of the fire in *The Girls of Slender Means* lies less in
Selina's concern to save the Schiaparelli dress—she sacrifices no
one to it—than in the fact that Joanna's hips are too wide to
permit her to escape in time. Hips too wide, the skylight
bricked up, only a slit of lavatory window available . . . If
evil exists and is active (not *only* in or from man), then some
sort of force for good must also exist, since evil has not prevailed
completely as yet. This near-Manichaean view could, today, be
held an argument for joining the Church, in the hope that you
will be throwing your weight, however slight it may be, on
the right side. The fire leads Nicholas to observe that 'a vision
of evil may be as effective to conversion as a vision of
good': which is likely to remind us of the earlier comment of an ageing spinster of slender means—'The Beatific
Vision does not appear to *me* to be an adequate compensation
for what we miss'. At all events, Mrs Spark neither despises
nor hates her fellow humans nor dotes simple-mindedly
on her Catholicism, her putative possession of the one and
only truth. What emerges, more visibly in *The Mandelbaum*

C

Gate than elsewhere in Mrs Spark, is a chastened Christianity not so far removed in matters of this world from the chastened humanism which is the only sort of humanism our age can allow.

The Mandelbaum Gate conducts us into a more public territory, a wider world, than we associate with Mrs Spark, though one as rich in intrigue as ever. Its heroine, Barbara Vaughan, is an English convert to Catholicism, half-Jewish, who is touring the Holy Land and also planning to meet her lover, an archaeologist working on the Dead Sea excavations in Jordan. Since she had first visited the Israeli part of Jerusalem, she is in some danger of arrest as a spy when she crosses to the Jordanian side and her half-Jewishness becomes known. Eventually (and perhaps more complicatedly than is strictly necessary) she is smuggled back into safety, with the help of various disguises, stolen clothes and a purloined passport, and through the efforts of diverse individuals, Jews, Arabs, Christians, Moslems, and even a mild British Foreign Office man——whose gallantry and enterprise in the affair are subsequently attributed to sunstroke, but never mind, he has had his day. Interwoven with Barbara's adventures is the story of an Arab-nationalist, Fascist, anti-Jewish conspiracy involving a second British diplomat and his wife. Paradox is insistent throughout the novel. Thus Barbara's pilgrimage is both sacred and profane. She describes herself as 'a Gentile Jewess, a private-judging Catholic, a shy adventuress'—and yet feels 'all of a piece'. Beersheba, the birthplace of Jacob, has a Detective Agency. The Holy Land is scattered with English flowers. Among the human creation, the irresponsible are to be trusted, the responsible are not, friends turn into enemies, enemies into friends. There is no art to find the mind's construction in the face, in the profession, the class, the race, the religion. A British diplomat is spying for Nasser. . . .

The question of 'commitment' lies at the heart of this novel, commitment to a faith or doctrine, political or religious or racial. And it almost looks as if, in this context of raging religions, obsessive politics and racial confrontations, the author's sympathies are with the non-committed, with 'the young or the young in heart who belonged to nothing but themselves', who meet in the cellar of a laundry at Acre (crusaders without a crusade? At any rate, another of Mrs Spark's little secret societies), 'lapsed Jews, lapsed Arabs, lapsed citizens, runaway Englishmen, dancing prostitutes, international messes, failed painters, intellectuals, homosexuals'. The leading spirits are Abdul and Mendel, 'fiery-eyed with a sense of portentous utterance', who chant together in a mixture of Arabic and Hebrew:

> It's all a long time ago. Great is the God of Israel! Mighty is Allah! We dance and sing and make love with each other, it is better than all that religion and hatred all the day long . . .

'Uncommitted' isn't the right word, however, since 'Being what thou art, lukewarm, neither cold nor hot, thou wilt make me vomit thee out of my mouth'. Rather, Mrs Spark would seem to be saying, hope lies with those who, though committed to a faith, preserve their 'private-judging' individualities, and are able to respect other individuals who are otherwise committed—persons like Abdul, and his sister Suzi who is chiefly responsible for Barbara's safe return, an Arab and Moslem for whom it is quite impossible, wholly ludicrous, to hate or despise somebody for being a Christian or a Hebrew, white or black. She praises the Bible, incidentally, for its obscurity: 'You can read two or three times, and you can find different opinions as to meaning.' Suzi is the best-beloved of the novel, and there is nothing of condescension in Mrs Spark's attitude towards this child of nature. Indeed both Suzi and Abdul at times speak with a disconcerting precocity, an improbable articulateness, as if filled with the Holy Ghost. Heaven will certainly have to find room for Suzi: like Abdul's father's house at Jericho, which harbours tourists, business contacts, paying guests, prostitutes, spies, refugees and lovers, it will need to have many mansions, furnished in a variety of styles.

The rough side of Mrs Spark's tongue is not to the fore in this affectionate and catholic novel. If anyone gets it, it is usually a Catholic, an English priest for being pedantic at the Altar of the Nailing of the Cross or Barbara for being priggish. This of course is not a new phenomenon, Mrs Spark often permits her characters to voice the standard objections to

Roman Catholicism, and occasionally a less common objection. 'Only people who did not want to think for themselves were Roman Catholics,' according to Miss Brodie. Sandy, who denounces Miss Brodie as a Fascist, later enters the Catholic Church, in whose ranks she finds 'quite a number of Fascists much less agreeable than Miss Brodie'. Probably Mrs Spark would sympathise with the man in *Memento Mori* who says, 'the more religious people are, the more perplexing I find them', and possibly with old Nelly Mahone of *The Ballad of Peckham Rye*, 'who had lapsed from her native religion on religious grounds', though perhaps she might feel that Ronald in *The Bachelors*—'as a Catholic I loathe all other Catholics'—goes a little too far.

Barbara's lover, a non-Catholic and divorced, is trying to get his marriage annulled by Rome, but it is practically certain that he won't succeed. Mrs Spark is perhaps a little too pleased with her familiarity with the inner workings of Catholic doctrine and procedure, and the lay reader at times feels excluded, but happily not for long. By a characteristic piece of Sparkian tricksiness, Barbara is made to announce that she has 'gone off' Harry. It turns out, though, that this public profession was designed to throw interested parties off the scent, and all along Barbara has intended to marry her lover, whatever the verdict of Rome, and in full knowledge of what this will mean to her as a Catholic. Her cheerfulness on this score, it must be said, is hardly the kind of thing one would expect from the heroine of a Catholic Novel. Her cheerfulness is rewarded. By an extra twist of tricksiness, Barbara's jealous girl-friend seeks to ensure that Harry's marriage will not be annulled by forging a birth certificate which makes him out a baptised Catholic—instead of a christened Methodist. 'The Romans do not allow divorce.' But nor do they recognise a marriage incurred outside the Church by one of its members, and the annulment is at once granted. Another paradox, and yet, as a priest remarks, 'all perfectly logical, really'.

Mrs Spark casually assures us that Rome would be perfectly content with a photographic copy of the supposed birth certificate, but the non-Catholic reader, with his customary respect for Rome's famous acumen and thoroughness, may still have his doubts . . . Is Mrs Spark actually an undercover agent concerned to bring the Church of Rome into contempt and disrepute? Or is she illustrating Rome's equally famous cunning, its worldly wisdom, whereby all that matters is that the couple should *believe* that Harry's first marriage is truly invalid? We know that Rome is deep and subtle, and that its labourers *in partibus intellectualium* are quite prepared to skate on the brink of heresy for the good of the cause. Sœur Sourire tells us that heaven is an *interesting* place, Antony and Cleopatra will be there, not to mention Diogenes and Professor Picard. . . But sooner or later the line is drawn, the axe descends, the sheep are separated from the goats. Whereas, even as a species of *jongleur de Notre Dame*, Mrs Spark's antics are a little on the equivocal side.

The Mandelbaum Gate would make an exciting and colourful film. The writing is less sophisticated, less pert, than in previous books, while remaining crisp, lively and to the point. Indeed, Mrs Spark permits herself a degree of crudeness here. The reference to the young Israeli who gets into trouble for dragging a spare part over the border to an Arab farmer whose tractor has broken down—this might be objected to, especially by those who admire Mrs Spark's customary finesse, as all too grossly 'symbolic'. But when a writer is dealing with real people or real countries or actual situations he had better be willing to acknowledge the inartistic thing, the excessively 'artistic' thing, which actually happens. It is very possible that a father did kill his son at the battle of Towton Field, and a son did kill his father. And in any case the only perceptible effect that fear of the banal has had on contemporary writing is one of enervation and trivialisation.

'Knots were not necessarily created to be untied,' Barbara reflects towards the end. 'Questions were things that sufficed in their still beauty, answering themselves.' And we think of the unanswered questions in Mrs Spark's novels. What were the voices Caroline heard in *The Comforters*, and was Georgina Hogg a witch? Who made the telephone calls in *Memento Mori*? Why did Sandy 'betray' Miss Brodie to the educational authorities? In *The Ballad of Peckham Rye* is Dougal Douglas the devil, and if so, why isn't he more devilish? It is a tribute to the sheer entertainment-value of Mrs Spark's writing that these unanswered questions don't worry us as much as we would have supposed—and a tribute to some of her admirers that they should have managed to find ingenious answers to them. But there is less of the coterie about *The Mandelbaum Gate*, less of the cabal and of the cabbalistic. By setting his action on the Israeli-Jordanian border, an author deprives himself of certain liberties he could have taken were it located in Peckham Rye. With reality breathing down her neck, Mrs Spark is in fact less inclined to leave the knots tied, the questions unanswered. The bullets that whizz across the border do rather mar the still beauty of the Holy Land—and sometimes they hit people. Life is dangerous enough, and sufficiently mystifying, and so are humans, without bringing in mysterious voices or black magic or witches or diamond-smuggling grannies. Though it may be her least idiosyncratic work, *The Mandelbaum Gate* seems to me Mrs Spark's best, her richest and most solid novel so far. (1965)

A MODERN DISEASE

Anthony Burgess's Shakespeare

WS, a young Stratford glover 'sold into kidskin slavery', experiences intimations of immortality, a vision of a goddess, in a bed chamber 'smelling of all the Indies'. The goddess is very woman, and the muse too, promising that his mouth will 'grow golden and utter speech for which the very gods waited and would be silent to hear'. Unfortunately, while blind drunk, WS is seduced by an old hand, Anne Hathaway, and then shot-gunned into marrying her, though he is really in love, really in real love, with another Anne, the Anne Whateley whose name is linked with his in the Bishop of Worcester's Register. WS clears off to London to repair the family fortunes, and falls in with (and in a sort of love with) Master WH, the young Southampton. Southampton's mother fees him to write sonnets for the young lord commending marriage, but his heart isn't in it. Later he makes the acquaintance of a dark lady, a very dark lady, rumoured to have been brought back as a child from the East Indies by Drake, who speaks Malay, and English with a taking accent: she is an admirer of Burbage, whom she has seen in *Rich Hard de Turd*. As sonnet 130 has it,

> *I love to hear her speak, yet well I know*
> *That music hath a far more pleasing sound.*

Here the novelist follows up G. B. Harrison's theory that the dark lady was a Negro prostitute called Lucy Negro, or the Abbess of Clerkenwell.

Time for a tiger? This tigress (portrayed compellingly, enormously, as one would expect from Anthony Burgess) robs WS of his time and much more, indeed a very rare mistress. Something of a snob, she is ambitious to meet the gentry, and before long Southampton has appropriated her from his poet:

'a sort of cuckolding', muses WS. Later WS rides to Stratford, to see New Place for the first time, and catches his wife in the act and the second-best bed with his younger brother, Richard. Again cuckolding drives him to the theatre and work. But there is to be one last grand confrontation with the dark Indonesian. (Who in the meanwhile has been delivered of a son, either Southampton's or WS's: so much, perhaps, for those Malayan pupils of Mr Burgess's who complained that Shakespeare had nothing to give to the East.) Lying on her bed, drunk, impotent, WS dreams of the erection of the Globe, and awakes to find an erection of a different sort, 'a playhouse from a tangled garden'. But this—the enemy in the blanket? —results in the pox, 'a hundred ulcers pitched their tents on my skin', and the final transformation of sweet Master Shakespeare into the author of the great unsweet plays. The goddess visits him and in a quasi-sexual encounter ('the rupturing of a hymen unknown to anatomists') releases upon him the promised vision, a vision of evil, not of wrong but of original evil.

> He thought that the great white body of the world was set upon by an illness from beyond, gratuitous and incurable. And that even the name Love was, far from being the best invocation against it, often the very conjuration that summoned the mining and ulcerating hordes. We are, he seemed to say, poisoned at source.

Nothing like the Sun is a clever, tightly constructed book, reminiscent in its much smaller and more sensational way of Mann's *Doctor Faustus*, full of the author's old verbal ingenuity (with something of Shakespeare's to boot), and likely to be one of the most remarkable (if most ambiguous) celebrations of the Bard's quatercentenary—although what it celebrates is pretty clearly something other than the Bard. It is a *tour de force*: a little too much force has been applied, in the wrong places. Mr Burgess has set himself so awesome a task that it seems hardly proper to complain at all. Only a gifted word-boy could have managed an Elizabethan-style idiom which most of the time strikes one as simply good lively English, if rather gamy. Of minor false notes there are few. Perhaps WS's mother's irritation with the mooning young poet couldn't be dispensed with: 'There sits he with idle versing and naught else in his head. What money will that ever bring in?' And incidentally it was a nice touch to make sister Joan the original of the greasy girl who keeled the pot, except that it would have been an even nicer touch to have a nice English girl or nice other sort of girl somewhere in the record. The old witch's prognostication—'You will take your pen and write like a clerk. You will be pushed and hurried and told to write with speed'—sounds as if WS is to grow up to be a reviewer (or would only a reviewer have such a thought?).

But mostly Mr Burgess is marvellously discreet and yet rich in his evocation of the contemporary background and his allusions to the poet's writings. There is something endearing about his scholarly jokes ('The Inns of Court, he thought, and the courts of inns; was there not perhaps some decent middle way, where poesy might be shouted at the world like truth itself?') and the rare manifestations of Professor Burgess: 'April 20th. Sir Philip Sidney's *Defence of Poesy* is out at last as a prin-ted book', or the affair of *Willobie his Avisa* ('You can expect talk now', WS tells Southampton), or the comments on *The Rape of Lucrece* and its 'stiffer and maturer view of virtue (not the seeming virtue of the innocent but the achieved virtue of the experienced)' as compared with *Venus and Adonis*.

The false note, it seems to me, is not a minor one, and it peals out full-bodiedly. In the case of a book subtitled 'A Story of Shakespeare's Love-life' it would be perverse to complain of the amount of sex present. But the point here is not the amount but the nature of it. Mr Burgess's narrative might help to account for the rougher bits in the Sonnets, for Lear's re-marks on the gentler sex, for Othello, Troilus, Leontes—but not for Hermione, Miranda, Imogen, Cordelia, nor exactly for that other dark lady, the serpent of old Nile. WS's sexual history—love-life seems hardly the word—is not so much grim or terrible as horrific and grotesque. His wife Anne 'was, he saw, hunting out corners of corruption in his soul which he had hardly guessed at before. . . .'. The corruption, to confine ourselves to the heterosexual, is carried further, flesh-crawlingly, by the dark Fatimah-Lucy. Then he catches his wife with his brother—and then the pox ('till my bad angel fire my good one out', perhaps). It is difficult to reconcile the works of Shakespeare with this WS, rather a poor stick, to whom things, chiefly shameful or horrid, are always being done. This is the sexual-melodramatic, or copulative grandguignolesque, comparable, as evidence of how Mr Burgess's judgment can occasionally desert him, to the spoiling of the powerful description of the hanging, drawing and quartering of Dr Lopez and company by one corny touch ('And then, *in articulo mortis*, his body spurted, but not with blood'), or the old husbands' tale of 'the land of women with their things cut at a strange slant'.

No doubt Shakespeare drank and saw the spider: but he saw other things too. Mr Burgess's vision of Shakespeare's vision is much more in the line of Mr Burgess's work than of Shakespeare's work. Thus Victor Crabbe of Mr Burgess's Malayan trilogy (still his best work) is left by his second wife, discovers that his beloved first wife (whom he killed in a car accident) had been unfaithful to him, is bitten in the foot by a scorpion and, stepping painfully on to a launch, falls into a jungle river and drowns unregarded. Spindrift in *The Doctor is Sick*, on the run from hospital, moneyless, hairless, shirtless, walks into the wrong hotel room and finds his wife in the act with an unknown man. The hero of *Honey for the Bears* loses his wife to a Russian lesbian, and his last words are

> You've sent me away nearly naked. Toothless, wifeless—ah, never mind. I don't even know what I am any more—sexually, I mean. Still, Shakespeare's sexual orientation is far from clear . . .

Julian Mitchell has recently remarked in the *London Magazine* that 'the typical Burgess protagonist is a teacher with a propensity towards infidelity, an impossible wife, and a capacity for suffering endless humiliation.' WS—who incidentally has tutored five young brothers in Gloucestershire and slept with one of them—fits wholeheartedly into this tradition, with no humiliation spared. 'My disease,' he says, 'was a modern disease.'

Whom Mr Burgess loveth, he chasteneth. But alas he flogs

them so savagely, with such ingenuity of violence and degradation, and with a little too much relish for there to be much love, that his readers are likely to rise up against him. Sorry for his battered creatures, they turn on the creator. It is unwise for an author to tyrannise—and rashest of all, perhaps, to tyrannise over our more than national poet. (1964)

ACCOUNT RENDERED

Truman Capote's *In Cold Blood*

O N 15 November 1959, in the village of Holcomb, in
Western Kansas, an entire household of four people,
father, mother, 16-year-old daughter and 15-year-old son,
were shot to death with a gun held close to their faces. The
father had previously had his throat cut. Otherwise the family
were not molested; indeed, the murderer or murderers had gone
to some little trouble to make them comfortable during their
last moments. Mr Clutter kept his money in the bank, not in
the house, and the total proceeds from this small massacre were
later estimated at between thirty and forty dollars—'a few
dollars and a radio'.[1]

The aplomb with which the operation had been carried out,
together with an apparent lack of resistance on the part of the
two sturdy Clutter males, suggested that the killers were
familiar with the Clutters and familiar to them. Yet anyone
who knew Mr Clutter at all would know that he was an en-
thusiast for cheques and kept next to no money on his person
or in the house. It would therefore seem to be a grudge-killing,
probably aimed at Mr Clutter and prudentially including the
other members of the family. The problem now was to find
the grudge, for quite plainly the Clutters were people whom no
one could possibly hate. They were virtuous, hard-working,
religious, kindly, modest and, in the case of the younger
generation, healthy, attractive and vivacious. They had not an
enemy in the world. None the less they had been murdered,
and so, since suspicion had to fall somewhere, it fell on Bobby
Rupp, Nancy Clutter's boy-friend, who might be thought to be
less than totally well-disposed towards Mr Clutter in that the
latter, a Methodist, had warned Bobby, a Catholic, that his
friendship with Nancy could never lead to anything 'serious'.
But it was less a question of proving Bobby's guilt than of

[1] *In Cold Blood*, by Truman Capote.

establishing his innocence, and this didn't take long, happily, since Bobby seems to have been more deeply, more personally, distressed by the murders than anyone else.

Perhaps the adult Clutters were not especially loved, but they were universally admired and respected. They had made good, and they *were* good; pre-eminently, they had achieved 'security'. And hence the immediate public terror caused by their murder: the least murderable people in the world, if they could be murdered, then anyone could be murdered. That, far from resisting, Mr Clutter treated the intruders with courtesy was possibly due to his sheer incredulity on that same point. 'That family represented everything people hereabouts really value and respect, and that such a thing could happen to them —well, it's like being told there is no God,' a local schoolmistress was impelled to observe. 'It makes life seem pointless. I don't think people are so much frightened as they are deeply depressed.' True, the events of 15 November must have drawn the attention of the Bible Belt ranchers to an aspect of God's wonders which may not have loomed large in their everyday Christianity. Depressed they might be, but that they were frightened too is indicated by the run on locks and bolts in the local hardware stores.

The prompt exculpation of Bobby Rupp kept the mystery a perfect mystery, and attempts by fellow-citizens to impair it —perhaps Clutter wasn't as sound financially as everybody thought and had killed his family and then himself, or perhaps the murderers mistook the Clutters for the Jones's, a considerably richer family living nearby—were pathetically ineffective. They were left with the thought, 'There, but for the grace of God . . .', and who could have been better candidates for that grace than the Clutters? It only remained to fix locks and bolts, to leave the lights blazing in the farmhouses all through the night, even to sell up one's property and move out of the county, out of the state. Human kind cannot bear very much mystery.

Quite rightly, *In Cold Blood* doesn't take the form of a mystery story, for the two proleptic murderers are introduced after only nine pages of concentrated description of Holcomb and of River Valley Farm and its owner, Herbert William Clutter. Thereafter, brief scenes of the Clutters living their last everyday day on the spot alternate with shots of Dick Hickock and Perry Smith, in a black 1949 Chevrolet sedan, on their way from Olathe, Kansas, to Holcomb, four hundred miles distant. The ancient cinematic technique is vindicated here, not so much by the building up of suspense (nausea is what is being built up), as by the fact that the intense worthiness of the Clutters requires them to be administered in smallish doses. '*De mortuis . . .*': our normal willingness in this point is meanly discouraged by the consideration that no one could find anything but good to say of them while they were living.

The Clutter homestead was innocent of a single ashtray, and the hired men on River Valley Farm were obliged to sign a contract containing a clause which rendered employment instantly terminated if the employee should be discovered 'harbouring alcohol'. In return, it should be said, Mr Clutter paid good wages and frequent bonuses. Quite simply, it paid to be good. Clearly the Clutters were not too good to be true, since Mr Capote convinces us of his truthfulness. But perhaps— with the possible exception of Nancy, who one feels would have married Bobby, despite God, despite Mr Clutter—perhaps they were too good for this world? Yet they were certainly not too good for *that* world, and Mr Clutter emerges as a culture-hero of the Bible Belt, not to be faulted either by worldly or by spiritual standards, for he had laid up moth-proof treasure on both levels. Yet it might be felt that the Clutters, eminently successful, wholeheartedly accepted by their world, were precisely the people to attract Hickock and Smith, against all likelihood, against all 'reason', to draw them across Kansas and to be murdered by them, by these two young men, eminently unsuccessful, rejected by their world. Some of us might take refuge in the thought that in fact the Clutters were eminently murderable, unlike you and me. But plainly this consideration would not be valid in Finney County where the Clutters were just good people, a good family in a good community, *primus inter pares*, and thus a little less murderable than Finney County's you and me.

After the discovery of the murders, Mr Capote naturally devotes the bulk of his attention directly to Smith and Hickock, at close range, occasionally narrating through Al Dewey, the haunted representative of the Kansas Bureau of Investigation, and reverting frequently and briefly to the citizens of Holcomb and Garden City, the county seat. This latter procedure serves to keep the Clutters alive in our minds, and especially to re-vivify and intensify the ghastly sense of waste, notably of the life, the liveliness, of Nancy Clutter. Without such reminders, we might, in the face of the almost suffocatingly detailed his-tories of Smith and Hickock that now ensue, even forget the victims, the other victims, which would trivialise the book without doing the murderers any sort of good. Perhaps in the later part of the book Mr Capote's prime problem was to pre-serve from oblivion the fact that murderers actually murder people, that four lives were ended on 15 November 1959 as well as two lives on 14 April 1965. The 'what' counts as well as the 'why': immersed in the pitiful black poetry of love-lessness, delinquency and crime, we can all too easily dismiss the murderees as dumbly insolent provocateurs, sheltering beneath their upright domesticity like people sheltering under a tree during a thunderstorm.

The Clutter affair would have remained a mystery but for a young man called Floyd Wells, then serving a sentence in Kansas State Penitentiary. When Wells read about the crime in the newspapers he knew at once who had committed it. Eleven years earlier he had worked on River Valley Farm. 'I liked Mr Clutter as much as any man I ever met . . . A nice family, *real* nice. I never forgot them.' The more was the pity, seeing that Wells told his cell-mate, Richard Hickock, about the Clutters, about their home and about a non-existent safe in Mr Clutter's office. Hickock told him that as soon as he was released he would join up with Perry Smith, already out on parole, and the two of them would make for Holcomb and 'tie them people up and gun them down'. The identity of the murderers having being revealed, it didn't take the FBI long to prove their guilt.

Both Hickock and Smith were remarkably articulate (no doubt Mr Capote was a persuasive listener), intelligent far above the average and particularly shrewd in judging each other. Hickock, as Mr Capote sees him, is markedly the less interesting of the two, the less to be felt for. He came from a 'semi-poor' but decent family, Smith from a bad, unloving one, his father a cowboy (Irish at that) and his mother an Indian (Cherokee). Smith was a book-lover, a romantic, a dreamer, and for him the purpose of the crime was to obtain money for treasure-hunting in Mexico or to buy a boat there and sail to Japan; he was 'an incessant conceiver of voyages'. Hickock was literal-minded, with no taste for poetry or music, but Smith admired him for his supposed practicality, his masculinity. Hickock had been twice married, twice divorced, and was the father of three boys; now, at 28, he was drawn to little girls. He later stated that for him the object of the Clutter project was to rape the daughter. Smith, who had a horror of what he called 'pervertiness', only prevented this by threatening to fight him. 'That's something I despise. Anybody that can't control themselves sexually. Christ, I hate that kind of stuff.' As for Hickock's practical nature, it was still left to Smith to kill the Clutters. Hickock was the smooth blusterer, enjoying power over others, sexually aggressive yet insecure. Smith was the edgy dreamer, bitter at his lack of education, an autodidact, a half-breed, quick to take offence if he suspected people thought him inferior. Both men had had bad car accidents; Smith was left with scarred and stunted legs which he hated anyone to see, and Hickock had since suffered from blackouts and fierce migraines.

Both of them were perfectly able to tell right from wrong, so there could be no appeal to the McNaghten Rules. It was simply that, except in certain particulars such as Smith's disapproval of 'pervertiness', there didn't seem to them all that much difference between right and wrong, not enough for the distinction to be significant. Like everyone else, they found themselves liking and respecting the Clutters; that even so they killed them without compunction was due as much to their contempt for life as to the instinct to preserve their own lives. 'The Clutters never hurt me. Like other people. Like people have all my life,' Smith said. 'Maybe it's just that the Clutters were the ones who had to pay for it.'

According to an interview recently printed in *The New York Times Book Review*, Mr Capote feels that contemporary novelists are 'too subjective . . . enraptured by their navels, and confined by a view that ends with their own toes.' He himself has felt the need 'to escape my self-created world', and *In Cold Blood*, following up the light-hearted reportage of *The Muses Are Heard*, is his contribution to a new literary form which he calls 'the non-fiction novel'. I doubt that his achievement is as new as he believes, but certainly to submit yourself to *In Cold Blood* is to undergo a lacerating experience. Mr Capote is careful to stay out of the book; he maintains a highly judicious tone in describing the McNaghten Rules, for instance, and he doesn't actually *say* that he is opposed to capital punishment. The book grew out of five years of research—and the sharing of other people's lives (Perry Smith left the author all his few worldly belongings)—and Mr Capote proceeds with such steady conviction that we would hardly query his liberal use of direct speech even without his assurance that his aim was to be 'immaculately factual', that there were witnesses to everything he reports and that Hickock 'had an absolutely fantastic memory—one of the greatest memories I have ever come across'.

And so we always know what Smith and Hickock are eating ('each chomping on two and a half sticks of Doublemint') or which tune Smith is singing to his guitar ('he knew the lyrics of some 200 hymns and ballads'). This is the sort of documentation one looks for from a novelist, and the psychiatrists' reports, though they may contribute to the air of 'authenticity', tell us nothing that we hadn't already understood from Mr Capote's use of the direct method. Apart from a few such over-earnest gestures towards 'non-fiction', the book's only defects lie in the distracting attention given to the other men awaiting execution along with Hickock and Smith and the curiously novelettish asides of the 'little did he know' variety sprinkled over the opening sections. 'Then, touching the brim of his cap, he headed for home and the day's work, unaware that it would be his last.'

Pathos of the most whole-hearted sort is not altogether out of order here. Sue, Nancy's friend, attends the auction of the Clutters' belongings and wishes she could buy Nancy's horse, 'big, fat Babe, who was much beyond her prime'. As Babe is led out of the corral, Sue 'ran forward, she raised her hand as

D

though to wave goodbye, but instead clasped it over her mouth'. The Clutters were such that their young daughter *would* have a big fat horse for a pet, and a girl like Sue for a friend. The novelist, in his 'self-created world', would have avoided this state of affairs, but the writer of non-fiction, faced with the facts, must respect them, and moreover, faced with the flat impenetrable virtuousness of Mr Clutter, has to make an effort to keep the dead alive in his reader's mind. Mr Capote's own 'self-created' Herb Clutter would have been less like a wholemeal American myth, one feels.

It may be regretted that Truman Capote the artist manifests himself so infrequently in this 'non-fiction novel', for what seems his most likely appearance is tremendously effective: the two thin grey tomcats who patrol Main Street and Courthouse Square, scrutinising the grilles of parked cars for bits of dead birds caught there. 'Using their paws as though they are surgical instruments, the cats extract from the grilles every feathery particle.' Observing the cats from his cell, Smith is pained by their behaviour, 'because most of my life I've done what they are doing. The equivalent.' The symbolic significance of the cats seems quite different: unlike Smith and Hickock, they are creatures who have successfully adjusted to their environment, and their environment does their killing for them. The cats are the happy comedians of the book, the only comic touch in it if you exclude the discrepancy between the 600 dollars paid to the hangman and the 40-odd dollars grossed by Hickock and Smith.

In Cold Blood ends with Al Dewey, the investigator, encountering Sue at the graves of the Clutter family. Bobby Rupp has married, she tells him, a beautiful girl. She herself is apparently on her way to meet some boy, 'a pretty girl in a hurry, her smooth hair swinging, shining—just such a young woman as Nancy might have been'. Life goes on, people fall in love and marry, the wheat bends in the wind, and Dewey starts for home. Columbia Pictures have bought the book, but even so Mr Capote didn't have to provide so outrageously banal a fade-out. At the same time, life does in fact go on, in non-fiction if not in the best fiction. And conversely it is true that in the midst of life we are in death. The citizens were quite right.

If there are people like Hickock and Smith in the world, and there are, if the world is such as to produce people like Hickock and Smith, and it is, then anybody can be murdered, even the Clutters. You don't need to be a millionaire, a politician, a film star, a crook—you merely have to be there. What happened to the Clutter family resembled an Act of God—as Dewey reflected, 'the victims might as well have been killed by lightning'—but behind it were the accumulated acts, actions and inactions, of a lot of people, by no means all of them documented even by the assiduous Mr Capote. The moral is an old and banal one: no man is an island. (1966)

BLOSSOMS AND BLOOD

On Knut Hamsun

THE Norwegian novelist Knut Hamsun made two visits to the United States in his youth, and after the second, between 1886 and 1888, he wrote *The Cultural Life of Modern America* (1889).[1] Otherwise a book over which a decent veil had best be dropped, it contains an eccentric critique of Shakespeare:

> There is a brutal simplification in Shakespeare's depiction of human emotions that makes them quite different from our own: his portrayals of love, wrath, desperation, and merriment fail to come off from sheer violence. We recognize these uncompromising emotions without shading or nuance as belonging to a bygone age when men still frothed at the mouth—consequently Shakespeare is not a modern psychologist. . . Shakespeare's plays are again just as simple, just as uncomplicated as the emotions he portrays; they are very often naïve in comparison with the work of modern dramatists.

This of course is a lot of balderdash, and it isn't the occasional kindly qualification ('Shakespeare is not a modern dramatist, but a dramatist he will remain until the end of time') that makes it almost acceptable in its context. It is the context itself which makes Hamsun's reflections on Shakespeare seem, relatively, high praise: for instance, if I may twitch the veil momentarily, he tells his shuddering readers how America attempted to create an intellectual élite by marrying its sons and daughters to imported Negroes ('a nascent human form from the tropics') and established instead 'a mulatto stud farm'.

The comments on Shakespeare may provide a point of departure for one's reflections on Hamsun's novels. He is an

[1] *The Cultural Life of Modern America*, by Knut Hamsun, edited and translated by Barbara Gordon Morgridge.

author whom it is difficult to write about without either under-
praising or overpraising. On the face of it, overpraising would
seem the more unlikely outcome, for there are passages in his
work ripely redolent of late nineteenth-century high-minded
flummery, but I note that (in an essay which does contain some
apt appreciation) Isaac Bashevis Singer makes sizable claims
for him: 'The whole modern school of fiction in the twentieth
century stems from Hamsun, just as Russian literature in the
nineteenth century "came out of Gogol's greatcoat".' This calls
to mind Hermann Hesse, another charmer of youth, who is
held to be a master of modernism, though to me his work resembles an intellectual supermarket in which some of the more
exciting elements of modernism can be obtained at less mental
expense than is asked in the studios of the great masters.

There is a faint flavour of the fairy-tale about Hamsun's
novels. What quickly strikes the reader is the somewhat
capricious way in which his characters respond to common
circumstances and the apparent gratuitousness of their behaviour. All this inevitably causes one to cock an ear for the
clash of symbols. Hamsun must surely find new readers at
a time when so many reject finished, 'autonomous' art in
favour of a malleable artlessness which they can shape to
accommodate their own inchoate yearnings and dissatisfactions.
But Hamsun, I would say, doesn't push his luck, he is a more
modest writer than Hesse, a more naïve one. Fundamentally
he is a slightly unexpected mixture of romantic and realist,
and while the romantic ingredients must appeal to both as-
piring youth and house-bound middle age—much as Hesse
does with his beckoning to the mysterious East—his realism
serves as a brake; the price for following one's star, for 'being
oneself', is pretty plainly chalked up. If they do not actually
kill themselves, his characters are generally tending towards
suicide, but he would not need to feel, with the author of *The
Sorrows of Young Werther*, that he was seducing the young and
had better supply a warning postscript: 'Be a man and do not
follow me'.

If Shakespeare's characters—Cleopatra, Leontes, Hamlet—
are 'brutally simple' in their emotions, then how very complex
must be Hamsun's characters, his psychology! Yet 'complex'

would hardly seem the unquestionably right word for them, even if, compared with the flat bovine faces of the human back-drop provided, they are discernibly unconventional. Pride would appear to be the chief serpent in the Earthly Paradise: yet—the novels lead us to ask—without this serpent, would there be any paradise? Hamsun is masterly above all in his dealings with young love, the power of love to obsess and possess and also its power for undoing itself. Yet however aptly Hamsun illustrates this theme in *Pan*[1] and in *Victoria*,[2] there is nothing *complex* about either the theme or his protagonists. We may feel that the latter are obstinate and unreasonable, that really there was nothing a quiet chat or an interchange of explanatory letters couldn't have put right, and that by arrogantly asking everything they are inviting nothing. This is not complexity, nor is it a triumph of 'shading or nuance': it is a long way off what Tieck called the 'beautiful contradictions' in Shakespeare's characters, that surface appearance of a penetrating, sensitive and essentially naturalistic expression of the workings of the human soul.

Even so, *Mysteries*[3] goes some way to living up to its title, while being probably the most humorous of Hamsun's novels. Johan Nilsen Nagel, the mysterious stranger, never reveals who he is or why he has come to the small coastal town. 'What right do you have to meddle in other people's business?' he asks himself. 'Why did you come here in the first place?' It is a mystery to him, too, though he has every appearance of knowing what he is up to, going about his mysterious business in a very business-like fashion. It is hard to tell whether he is surreptitiously doing good or surreptitiously doing ill in the guise of surreptitiously doing good. Like other Hamsun characters—like the young writer in *Hunger*, though he rarely has anything to give—Nagel is a compulsive giver-away of money, his manner of giving ranging from the most exquisitely considerate to the most arrogantly rude. Also the most humorous, as when he contrives laboriously to pay a poor woman a ridiculously generous price for a worm-eaten old chair. 'If it

[1] *Pan*, translated by James W. McFarlane.
[2] *Victoria*, translated by Oliver Stallybrass.
[3] *Mysteries*, translated by Gerry Bothmer.

were up to you, what would prevent you from asking three hundred crowns . . . You would be justified since you know we are discussing a rare and valuable piece. But I wouldn't pay a fantastic price like that . . . I'll give you two hundred for it and not a shilling more.' She wants him to take the chair for nothing, but he gets round this by making her promise not to sell it to anyone else without first letting him know and then sending a third party to her with an offer of 220 crowns.

He also befriends The Midget, a poor misshapen and bullied creature, though not without bullying him himself. The proleptic shade of Ingmar Bergman lurks in the undergrowth. Possibly Nagel is mad: that is the diagnosis of a doctor offstage. Yet it seems that there is method in his madness, or there is about to be, at least until he falls in ill-conditioned love with the minister's daughter, Dagny, who is engaged to an absent naval officer. To Dagny, Nagel is 'the kind of man who is at odds with everybody and everything'. He is against pragmatism because it 'robs our life of poetry, dreams, mysticism'— and certainly dreams and reveries loom large throughout Hamsun—but he is also against poets ('a rash, a scab on society, purulent pimples') and other Great Men. Nagel is so much the individualist that he declines to be influenced even by other individualists. In an individual's life there is only room for one truly individual individual: himself.

Hence, or so it seems, the failure of the passionate lovers of the other novels, couples resembling Achilles and Penthesilea (though reduced sharply to a scale congruous with provincial Norwegian society of the time) in that one or other of them must die. But in fact and in effect is Nagel more than eccentric? His outbursts of humility are as immoderate as his outbursts of arrogance. Manic fits yield without much shading or nuance to depressive phases. He has distracted the townspeople, he claims: 'I've created one scandal after another in your dreary, conformist lives!' Then he rushes out and jumps into the sea: a fact not divulged to the townspeople, for whom he has vanished as suddenly and mysteriously as he came. Yes, he has given a small dull town something to talk about, a few very minor scandals. But nothing to justify the blurb's grand talk of 'a man

cursed with the merciless gift of unsparing insight into the
human soul, particularly his own; a man possessed by the
Nietzschean will for power and domination'. It would be
easier to see *Mysteries* as an amiable send-up of that famous
Nietzschean will: Nagel is an energetic busybody who can't
find anyone really worth dominating, except Dagny, and he
fails there.

'Tell me, am I behaving as you want me to?' Edvarda asks
the hunter Glahn in *Pan*, a book dedicated to 'Johan Nilsen
Nagel'. Individualists don't quite know how to behave towards
other individualists, and Hamsun's characters are creatures of
moods. They are also in one sense children of nature, happily
in love with nature, a love with which for a while they confuse
their human love. There is, in a less gratulatory sense, a peculiar
childishness about them. I should think even the most recep-
tive of readers must come to feel that their behaviour is often
wildly gratuitous, deliberately *difficile*, over and beyond the
call of individualism and truth to self. Like Nagel (who was
also his own best friend) they are themselves their own worst
enemies. Glahn causes the death of the girl who loves him—
her fault is that she is too truly a child of nature—and pines
for another who (it must be admitted) is something of a flirt.
When he departs, he makes Edvarda a present of his faithful
dog, as she has requested: that is, he shoots it and sends her the
body. Nagel poisoned Dagny's dog, but he had a reason of a
sort: the animal used to bark when he hung around her house at
nights. In the epilogue we learn of Glahn's death in India: it is
an indication of the difference between Hamsun and Hesse
that as far as we know Glahn went to India simply to hunt—and
to sulk.

Probably what is most impressive in *Pan*, most memorable,
is the keen evocation of the natural scene, the celebration of the
forest and its creatures. Though Marvell's 'Garden' is a hothouse by comparison, we may recall these lines from it:

> Such was that happy Garden-state,
> While Man there walk'd without a Mate:
> After a Place so pure, and sweet,
> What other Help could yet be meet!

Only man is—not exactly vile, but wilful, demanding, touchy. Nature's richness is present in *Victoria*, too, but love is the larger presence here, the book is more centrally a study in the varieties of love.

> Love was God's first word, the first thought that sailed across his mind. He said, Let there be light, and there was love. And every thing that he had made was very good, and nothing thereof did he wish unmade again. And love was creation's source, creation's ruler; but all love's ways are strewn with blossoms and blood, blossoms and blood.

Again, love goes wrong, but not in the horrific modern manner: on the contrary, *Victoria* is a romantic book, fornication-free, demonstrating that love is not necessarily born in bed and neither does it necessarily die there. All the same, the pride and the recognition of superiority which gave birth to love also, through the perversities of pride, bring it to its death. Victoria herself resembles Edvarda, but is more pathetic in her end. Johannes, the miller's son who becomes a famous writer, is a sturdier character than Glahn and a less eccentric one than Glahn or Nagel: he works, he survives because of his work, and the running-together in his mind of fantasy and reality is accountable for in a young writer. Johannes has what his creator had but neither Nagel nor Glahn was given—a profession, and one in which the imagination finds space to live and move with complete legitimacy.

The narrator of *Hunger*[1] has that same happiness—that richness, if no other. Love is only an interlude here, or perhaps only one hallucination among others. Here too the quirks and fancies are immediately explicable and apropos as well, since the protagonist is not only a young writer but, for much of the time, he is literally starving—as his creator had starved not long before. His behaviour is not gratuitous, nor are his fantasies: indeed the latter even manage to be humorous. Reduced to sucking on wood shavings, he imagines he is a cabinet minister ordering roast beef in a restaurant. He believes quite seriously that he will be able to pawn the buttons

[1] *Hunger*, translated by Robert Bly.

off his coat and goes about doing so with all a gentleman's casualness:

> Well, I have something here, and I wanted to ask you if you had any use for—something that was really in the way at home, you understand, no room for them, some buttons . . . Just enough for a cigar or whatever you think right. I was just going by anyway and thought I'd stop in.

In his extreme physical weakness he finds that some of his faculties are sharpened (he can tell that his landlady is pregnant) while others are blunted (he can't add up a simple bill). Life —or is it Society, or God?—may seem to be playing cat-and-mouse with him, for whenever he is about to go down for good, a few coins somehow drop into his hands. But what really sustains him is something else—a vivid if variegated inner life. Just as he has brought himself to swallow his pride and approach the stable-boy for the loan of a crown, the boy asks him for the loan of five crowns. The turn of events amuses him vastly:

> I threw myself down on the bed and laughed. What incredible luck that he asked me first! My honour was saved. Five kroner. God help us! You could just as well have asked me for five shares in the Steam Kitchen, or for an estate out in Aker.

And when in the closing pages he signs on a merchant-ship sailing to England, a naturalistic interpretation comes quite as readily as a symbolic one: he has made his point, he has proved that he can write, he has proved himself.

Of the novels published by Hamsun in the 1890's and recently (and well) translated or re-translated, *Hunger* and *Victoria* are the best as works of art, complete, finished and self-sufficient, while *Pan* offers the nature-lover some fine and large incidentals. But *Mysteries*, I would think, is likely to hold the greatest appeal at the present time, not merely because of the amused fondness we form for the disconcerting Johan Nilsen Nagel himself, but by virtue or by vice of the book's 'mysteriousness', its open-endedness, its open invitation to interpretation as you like it. (1971)

MAN OF BALANCE

The Letters of Thomas Mann

THE obvious comparison with Thomas Mann is Goethe—who but Mann could be compared with Goethe?—and the comparison stands even after one has remarked that Goethe was primarily a poet and Mann exclusively a novelist and essayist. What remains is a common sense of largeness (which some have found intimidating, others offensive), of representativeness, of 'Germanness' certainly but of much more as well. If one were required to take to that famous desert island the works of just one twentieth-century author, the author would have to be Thomas Mann.

Mann wrote of Goethe:

> He exercised a kind of universal dominion in the form of irony and serene betrayal of mutually exclusive points of view, one to the other. There was in this a profound nihilism; there was also art's —and nature's—objectivistic refusal to analyse and evaluate. There was an ambiguous impishness, and element of equivocation, negation, and all-embracing doubt which led him to make self-contradictory pronouncements.

Michael Hamburger claims that these words are much more true of Mann than of Goethe, 'who was deeply, instinctively certain about the things that mattered to him'. There is some justice in this, though I think that in his work Goethe is more complex and ambiguous than is here suggested, and Mann in the final count less equivocal, or no more equivocal than is inevitable in an author who was so 'meticulous and exhaustive' in his procedure, whose canvas was customarily so large in area and so minutely detailed. It is easy to be simple and straightforward in the limited art of the poster, and brief in the mode of the undemonstrated aphorism. Writing to Hermann Hesse in 1947, Mann said, 'Once again I perceive how nothing is really interesting except the incommensurable'. And perhaps it says something for him that he has been attacked both for failing to commit himself and for propagandising.

This new selection of letters[1] ought to increase the admiration of Mann's admirers. It may arouse a few self-doubts in those who complain about his 'non-commitment'. It will certainly antagonise further those who find offensive his wide-ranging mind, his inclusiveness, and his peculiar blend of solemn scholarliness with pervasive irony. Eliot's definition of wit is apropos here: 'a recognition, implicit in the expression of every experience, of other kinds of experience which are possible'; and I think it is the case that in Mann this wit or irony is 'sometimes stifled by erudition'. That irony should attend him in his most affectionate passages has proved a general stumbling-block. That elsewhere it has not invariably been detected has proved another.

To read these letters from the beginning is to feel that Mann was born an author, a man of letters in his cradle. The first letter here, written when he was 14, is signed 'Th. Mann, Lyric-dramatic author'; the second, a couple of months later, mentions that he is 'diligently reading Schiller's works, which I got for Christmas'; and the third, at the age of 19, is addressed to Richard Dehmel who had praised his first published story. It seems that the man (by nature, by birth, by breeding) and the time and the place had irresistibly coincided, and Europe was to have a major literary intellectual of 'representative' character and Goethean or Tolstoyan proportions. In fact, as it began, so it went on, through two wars and a lot of uneasy peace, this most substantial success story. It needs an effort to remember that two of Mann's sisters and one of his sons committed suicide, that for years he wrote in a language in which he was banned and from which he had to be translated, and that, though at every stage of his career he was acclaimed, he was also much abused.

He made what seems exactly the right marriage, too. The letters to Katia Pringsheim, written during her initial and not unnatural hesitation, are the most endearing here, and among the most revealing, for Mann didn't develop so much as expand.

[1] *The Letters of Thomas Mann, 1889-1955*, selected and translated from the German by Richard and Clara Winston.

I am cold-hearted, you must know . . . In all seriousness, there are no more than five or six persons in Germany who know what irony is, and understand that it need not necessarily stem from a desolate inner life.

But—or and—also:

. . . 'smartness' is something deeply nasty. The 'smart' person confines himself to eating no more than two rolls every day, lives cautiously, loves cautiously, and is too cautious to resolutely bind his life to his love . . .

And

A primitive and vital instinct tells me, in a kind of colloquial and unsophisticated language, that emotions of the sort I have for you cannot be in vain.

Such a man could hardly not become a public figure, even if events hadn't made him the greatest German writer in exile. Public and professional obligations loom immense in these pages: statements, refutations, centennial tributes, appeals (he did much to help émigrés less fortunate than himself), lectures and articles, counselling at every level from a GI up to the President of the United States. He was obliged to speak against much that was German (he made up his mind about Hitler at a very early stage), obliged to speak for other things that were German in other ways, obliged to speak on behalf of victims of Nazism—and then, when the war ended, it was demanded of him that he should speak up for those intellectuals who had managed to rub along with Nazism. It is a tribute to his moral and intellectual—and physical—strength that he maintained such a steady standard of intelligence, knowledgeableness and courage.

As if all this weren't real enough, the 'real' Thomas Mann went on living elsewhere; under the towering international public figure, the private character of the artist survived intact and vigorous. There is, it is true, some orotundity in these letters, unalleviated by irony or a tongue visibly in cheek, and those to his children seem to have been composed for some solemn public occasion: 'Why should I not admit that I am father enough to see in your development during these six hard years an example of the maturity which freedom can reach in exile?' Yet perhaps, for his children, it was an appropriate manner and aptly understood. Erika Mann's memoir, *The Last Year*, would not lead us to believe otherwise.

While admiring the dignified dexterity of Mann's performances on official occasions, we may think of his comment on Goethe: 'he is the greatest of them all because he so happily unites the daemonic and the urbane'. Dexterous in a more amusing fashion is his letter to Gerhart Hauptmann, judiciously blending formality, reverence and self-respect, in which he excuses and justifies himself for having used the dramatist as a model in creating his character Peeperkorn. 'I did wrong, but I was right'—and after all, despite 'the, let us say, ironic and grotesque artistic means which it is my wont to manipulate', Peeperkorn *is* a giant 'who dwarfs all babblers'. Ironic in a simpler mode is his letter to the President of the Gourmet Society of America in 1938 declining to attend a meeting of that body:

I was delighted with your statement that even the peoples of the East traditionally suspend hostilities while dining together, for this opens up the possibility of a considerable extension of the scope of work of your Society in places not so remote as the East.

Letters to Hesse and other kindred artistic spirits are professional in a different sense. In 1934, 'I am a man of balance. I instinctively lean to the left when the boat threatens to capsize on the right, and vice versa . . .' In 1951 he defends himself against such epithets as 'ponderous' and 'pompous':

The fact is that I consider myself primarily a humorist—and this kind of self-image is incompatible with Olympianism or pompousness. Humour, I am inclined to think, is an expression of amiability and comradeship towards those with whom we share this planet—in short, of fellow feeling, of an intention to do good to men, to teach them an appreciation of charm and to spread liberating merriment among them. Incidentally, it is more closely akin to modesty than to arrogance and conceit . . .

Erika Mann reports that his modesty often led him into incautiousness—he couldn't believe that people would attach such importance, one way or the other, to what he said or wrote. 'Comedy, laughter, humour seem to me more and more the soul's salvation': he was, as Michael Hamburger has said, 'a magnificent comedian'. Brevity, however, was hardly the soul of his wit.

Far from the public figure smothering the private one, the former could never have endured without the latter sustaining it from within. 'To write Thomas Mann's "Life" will probably always mean to write about his writings,' Erich Heller has said. 'For with him, living and writing were all but identical activities.' I think, though, that it will always be difficult to write about his writings. He was a great man, whose work enriches like that of no other novelist of our time. But it will still be difficult to defend him against charges arising out of his irony: charges of evasiveness, aestheticism and even callousness. At any rate, without representing his works as simpler than they are—and without representing oneself as simpler-minded than perhaps one is. (1970)

HESSE *VERSUS* HESSE

'ZWEI Seelen wohnen ach! in meiner Brust.' And very convenient it is for the writer, for one soul can bleed on the sleeve while the other gets up to other things in other places. It is not that the breast needs to be a specially large one to entertain two souls, but rather that those among whom the two-souled move may have to be remarkably broad-minded and long-suffering. Perhaps prepared to suffer long and very painfully indeed. I will not dwell on the lowest and most horrifying depths to which double-souledness can sink—Hans Magnus Enzensberger's exemplum of the concentration-camp commandant who plays Schubert sonatas when off duty will suffice —for Hermann Hesse was obviously a good man, a good-hearted man, who recognised the onset of Germany's Faustianity at a very early date and removed himself to single-souled Switzerland.

Hesse too loved music, but like Thomas Mann he had his misgivings about the German love of it. In *The Magic Mountain* (1924), Settembrini—liberal humanist, *homo humanus*, whose musical emblem would be nothing more sinister than the windbag or the barrel-organ—considers music 'politically suspect', and in *Doctor Faustus* (1947) the Devil points out that he ought to know something about music:

> Christian in reverse, as it were: introduced and developed by Christianity indeed, but then rejected and banned as the Divel's Kingdom . . . a highly theological business, music—the way sin is, the way I am . . . For there is true passion only in the ambiguous and ironic. The highest passion concerns the absolutely questionable.

Similarly in Hesse's *Steppenwolf* (1927) the ambiguous hero laments the hegemony which music exerts over the German spirit:

We intellectuals, instead of fighting this tendency like men and rendering obedience to the spirit, the Logos, the Word, and gaining a hearing for it, are all dreaming of a speech without words that utters the inexpressible and gives form to the form-less.

And so, he continues in one of those interesting discursive passages scattered through Hesse's work, the German spirit has intoxicated itself with beautiful sounds and

none of us intellectuals is at home in reality. We are strange to it and hostile. That is why the part played by intellect even in our own German reality, in our history and politics and public opinion, has been so lamentable a one.

A far cry from our good clean English music, food of love, soother of savage breasts, softener of rocks, bender of knotted oaks, and server of other social functions! But let us have done with the commandant and Schubert, and also with Enzens-berger's equally double-souled SS officer who carries Hölderlin (though a word-user and not a dreamer of music) in his knap-sack. Hesse's novels, and especially his largest and least readable, *Magister Ludi* ('The Glass Bead Game', 1943), are much nearer to the ivory tower than to the concentration camp, albeit an ivory tower which bustles with enigmatic activity. The 'Treatise on the Steppenwolf' pokes fun at Faust's pathetic claim, 'in a line immortalised among schoolmasters and greeted with a shudder of astonishment by the Philistine', to possess *two* souls:

The breast and the body are indeed one, but the souls that dwell in it are not two, nor five, but countless in number. Man is an onion made up of a hundred integuments, a texture made up of many threads.

Duality can be dull enough, but think of the potentialities of plurality! Why I compared Hesse's novels to ivory towers or palaces of philosophy is that customarily they *talk* a lot about man's many souls yet they rarely or only briefly *show* us any

E

one of these souls or selves in action. Thomas Mann is the greater novelist in that, though he too is ever ready for a long, abstract and learned excursus, he surrounds his lecturing with characters who are irresistibly 'flesh and blood'. Hesse, however, falls back on the 'the East', 'the ancient Asiatics', the Yin and the Yang, that unholy pair of twins, or points encouragingly to 'India' or 'China' (an India empty of Indians, a China without Chinese), or to the Buddha, or 'the return into the All'. *Magister Ludi* is an exhausting account of the minutiae of an aristocratic, highly spiritual secret society; the theme, much beloved of earlier German writers and categorised in the formula *Bundesroman* or 'League Novel', is treated also in *Demian* and *The Journey to the East*. But the odd thing about this secret society is that it doesn't *do* anything. It simply *is*. The secret is in the secret, perhaps.

Theodore Ziolkowski describes the book admiringly as an attempt on the grand scale 'to project the ideal into reality',[1] but the Magister himself retires from the Order because of its aestheticism, its ignorance of the outside world. In fact we see little of any 'commitment to life' *within* life and the outside world: this is only more highflown talk. When Magister Knecht leaves the Castalian Order, so Ziolkowski glosses, 'his representative life is over. He is now free to live or to die as an individual.' In the story he dies, pretty promptly. But then, life in Hesse is mostly a shabby business; he could never have achieved anything comparable to Thomas Mann's Mynheer Peeperkorn, ludicrous and majestic, gone to seed and full of seed, a symbol and a particular Dutch coffee-planter from Java, 'Life' itself and yet 'an out-and-out personality'. Mann sounds like a novelist, if discernibly a German one then the most 'Dickensian' of them, where Hesse sounds like a commentator on somebody else's novels, as when in *Magister Ludi* he instructs the reader that the Bead Game 'represented a select, symbolical form of the quest for perfection, a sublime alchemy, a self-approach to the inherent spirit beyond all images and pluralities—and thus to God'. Ziolkowski, a devotee writing at length on the master, carries the process of abstraction and rarefaction to the point at which the reader's (or this reader's) mind fails to get

[1] *The Novels of Hermann Hesse*, by Theodore Ziolkowski.

a foot-hold or a nail-hold on the discourse and can only suppose that the exegete speaks with the tongue of angels perhaps,
but certainly not with that fleshy muscular organ given to man.

Two at least of Hesse's novels are exceptions or partial exceptions to what I have said or implied above. I must have given
the impression that Hesse is an extreme case of Teutonic
heaviness and humourlessness, and yet *Steppenwolf* is quite funny
in some of its discursive passages and in some of its incidents.
Harry Haller, a lonely, wretched intellectual, pacifist and lover
of Mozart, 'a most refined and educated specialist in poetry,
music and philosophy', falls in with a strange and seemingly
bisexual dance-hostess called Hermine (Hermann). Hermine
takes his re-education or de-education in hand, makes him buy
a gramophone and some jazz records, teaches him to dance, and
generally introduces him to a new world. 'Marble-topped
tables, jazz music, cocottes, and travelling salesmen!' She also
provides him with an attractive mistress, Maria, who 'taught
me the charming play and delights of the senses' and brings
him to view less priggishly 'the world of the dance and pleasure
resorts, the cinemas, bars and hotel lounges'. The account of a
late flowering of sexual love is quite charming and tender, but
Harry somehow knows that this new life cannot last and some
new 'unwinding of fate' is at hand:

> It was my destiny to make another bid for the crown of life in
> the expiation of its endless guilt. An easy life, an easy death—
> these were not for me.

No such luck! In the course of the book's lively yet enigmatically
phantasmagoric denouement, Maria and Hermine disappear
and Harry is left with 'all the hundred thousand pieces of life's
game' in his pocket:

> A glimpe of its meaning had stirred my reason and I was deter-
> mined to begin the game afresh. I would sample its tortures once
> more and shudder again at its senselessness. I would traverse not
> once more, but often, the hell of my inner being.

In 1961 Hesse complained that *Steppenwolf* had been violently misunderstood, especially by its most enthusiastic readers who identified themselves with Harry in his sufferings and failed to realise that 'the story pictures a disease and crisis—but not one leading to death and destruction, on the contrary: to healing'. But it is the tale we have to trust; the sheer phantasmagoria of the ending and the obscure 'healing' which it is alleged to point towards simply cannot stand up to the weight of melancholy, the realistic and documented misery, of the book's first half.

I complained that we rarely saw any of Hesse's 'souls' or fragments of souls in action. Rare in that respect, then, is *Narcissus and Goldmund* (1930), which Ziolkowski describes as the most popular and most imperfect of Hesse's later novels, but which I would say is the best of all. The duality here is very plainly exemplified in Narcissus, the scholarly and austere monk, and Goldmund, the artist, adventurer and lover. It is Narcissus, as befits 'mind', who expounds with Hesse's customary explicitness the differences between the two of them. 'The difference between mother-heritage and father-heritage, the difference between soul and mind'; 'we are sun and moon, dear friend; we are sea and land'; 'you sleep at your mother's breast; I wake in the desert. Your dreams are of girls; mine of boys.' Where Narcissus looks to God the Father and teaches in the monastery school, Goldmund looks to the Earth-Mother and becomes a sculptor. Hesse spells out the message in large lettering, reminding us for instance that pain and joy resemble each other closely (we would like to remind Hesse that sometimes they don't, too), and that while it is good to lead a disciplined life of intellect, religion and meditation, it is also good (for all manner of thing shall be well, though some of us may not always think so) to 'suffer sun and rain, hunger and need, to play with the joys of the senses and pay for them with suffering'. Goldmund is brought back to the monastery and dies in Narcissus' arms, and to Narcissus is given the bulk of the moralising, the explication of the novel and the directing of the reader's intellectual responses. But the adventures are given to Goldmund, and it is these which count.

Ziolkowski complains that the title of the first English translation referred only to Goldmund, thus by implication ignoring the significance of the counterpart, Narcissus, and he quotes

Hesse's own protest against readers who made the same mistake:

> The book and its world become meaningless if one splits it like that: Narcissus must be taken just as seriously as Goldmund; he is the counterpole.

We will silence our doubts as to whether, in that case, the monk is altogether happily named, but again it is the tale we must trust, not what its author says about it. I maintain that the reader to whom this Narcissus can *mean* as much as this Goldmund must have come to the book with an entrenched predisposition in favour of thin-lipped philosophising and cloistered virtue and a gross lack of interest in the life of the world and the life of the senses. For one thing, if we agree to think of the two poles in question as 'Nature' and 'Spirit' (Ziolkowski's suggestion), then where Narcissus is spirit alone, we come to feel that Goldmund is both nature and spirit. Ziolkowski contends that something has gone wrong 'technically', and this he attributes to a structural flaw in the novel arising from the fact that Hesse conceived Goldmund before he conceived Narcissus and the former thus had an unfair start in life. I would say, though, that something has gone right—despite Hesse. (We should note that in *Siddhartha*, 1923, the most tract-like of the novels, the eponymous hero who has been a merchant, lady's man, epicure, gambler and ferryman, and who distrusts doctrines and teachers, ends up holier than his friend Govinda, ascetic monk and disciple of the Buddha.) Where generally Hesse's persons merely dent the walls of the ivory tower on the inside, here Goldmund breaks clean through them—and goes on what seems a *real* journey through a reasonably real medieval Germany.

Goldmund's adventures are largely erotic, and in a recent piece in *The New Republic* Stephen Koch remarked irreverently that what the novel is really about is not Artist *versus* Intellectual or what have you but 'wanting women'. Good for Goldmund, then, for he not only wants, he gets! His success rate is perhaps unrealistically high. 'Everywhere women desired him and made him happy . . . Without knowing it, he was to each woman

the lover she had wished for and dreamed of.' He begins to
feel that

> perhaps his destiny was to learn to know women and to learn
> love in a thousand ways, until he reached perfection, the way
> some musicians were able to play not only one, but three, four,
> or a great number of instruments . . . Here he had no difficulty
> learning; he never forgot a thing. Here experience accumulated
> and classified itself.

All the same, women don't stay with him very long, and the
two he most desires elude him altogether. But what impresses
is the *goodness* of the eroticism, its naturalness, indeed its
pleasurableness. This endows Hesse's accounts with an effect of
quite startling novelty at a time when the chief attraction of
much current fiction is its analysis of the repulsiveness of
physical intercourse. Goldmund enjoys making love to women,
women enjoy having Goldmund make love to them, and Hesse
knows how much of love-making can be justly conveyed
through words and how much cannot. His easy, sure touch in
physical matters (even the highly spiritual *Siddhartha* has some
wise remarks on the subject) contrasts oddly with his over-
heated metaphysicality, his lasciviously loose talk about destiny, the abyss, the longing for death and for the All.

But wanting and getting girls is not the whole of Goldmund's
adventures. He kills twice, under provocation. And to rectify
the balance further, Hesse follows Love with Sickness (the
scenes of the Black Death are stark enough but not manipulated
morbidly) and then with the persecution of the Jews in the
wake of the plague. In this book too he makes excessively free
with such large, question-begging concepts as 'the demands of
fate', but despite the author's assiduous and finally tedious
interventions, the balance of the novel's sympathy tips in
favour of nature, art, action and the flesh, as against spirit,
religion, contemplation and asceticism. The novel does have a
tapestried air about it, a faint but distinct smell of fake-medieval
allegorising, yet there is still more of the feel of life in it, of
experience not solely cerebral, than in any other work of
Hesse's.

Of the other books recently published in translation there is less to be said. *Rosshalde* (1914) is an essentially *gemütlich* mixture of idyll and anguish, of talk about life and talk about art, with some talk about the exotic East thrown in. The chief duality here seems to be the old one of life and art which Mann treated so much more comprehensively, pointedly and professionally.

> The intellect of man is forced to choose
> Perfection of the life, or of the work . . .

Johann Veraguth is a famous artist who hardly exists at all as a man. He resides on the beautiful estate of Rosshalde, coolly estranged from his family, which is only held together by Pierre, the 7-year-old son uneasily shared by the parents. Of Veraguth we are told plainly,

> he, who never sent a bungled drawing or painting out into the world, suffered deeply under the dark weight of innumerable bungled days and years, bungled attempts at love and life . . .

One of those beautiful, over-sensitive, precocious children who are too good to live, Pierre dies. And Veraguth prepares to leave for the East, where (he believes) he will be able to unite his art with a 'new life, which, he was resolved, would no longer be a groping or dim-sighted wandering, but rather a bold, steep climb'. New life will nourish new art: it is the old Gauguinesque dream. What is most convincing here is the harrowing account of the child's sickness and death, an event merely incidental to what is presumably the novel's central concern.

Demian (1919) is considered the 'break-through', the first of the maturely meaningful novels. I would say it is insufficiently cryptic for its own good. Hesse jeopardises the novel by tactlessly tying his vague prophecies to a particular occurrence, the First World War. Thus we hear of 'a great chain of events' commencing with the war, about 'a new world' which is beginning to emerge and 'something akin to a new humanity' which is taking shape 'deep down, underneath'—as it were, something like Wilfred Owen's 'Strange Meeting' without that poem's conditional tense and its elegiac tone and tenor. The novel's schoolboy pranks, quasi-mystical visions and ad-mixture of sexual stirrings account for its appeal to adolescents of all ages.

Halfway through *The Journey to the East* (1932) the narrator, H. H. (Harry Haller, Hermann Hesse), cries out, 'But how can it be told, this tale of a unique journey, of a unique communion of minds, of such a wonderfully exalted and spiritual life?' Towards the end, at a judicial assembly of the League, its Speaker announces that the League is ready to pass judgment on the narrator,

> who has now realised how strange and blasphemous was his intention to write the story of a journey to which he was not equal, and an account of a League in whose existence he no longer believed and to which he had become unfaithful.

The catch is that the League can only be spoken of in public by those who have left it, and those who have left it cannot re-member what the League was all about! Therefore, as Ziol-kowski puts it, all the narrator can do now 'is to narrate his own *attempt to narrate* the journey to the East: the act of narration has become the subject of the story'. Ending as it does with what is blatantly a symbol, but a symbol amenable to any number of interpretations, the book can be said to be open-ended. In that sense it can also be said to be open-beginninged and open-middled as well. It seems to me an amusing piece of higher chicanery (indeed it seems to me rather like a parodic send-up of *Magister Ludi* in particular and of armchair 'journeys' in general), but Hesse apparently took it very seriously, and there have been and no doubt are and will be plenty of readers ready and eager to supply their own beginning, middle and end, and in effect to write Hesse's book for him.

Beneath the Wheel (1906), Hesse's second novel, is more honest and more sad, the story of a gifted boy of humble birth who is sent from his village to a theological academy, sinks to the bottom of the class, breaks down, goes home, and dies. Ziolkowski claims that, just as the school is the same as the one in *Narcissus and Goldmund*, so is the duality of the later novel anticipated here in the school friendship between Hans Gieben-rath and Hermann Heilner (another H. H., though here a rather fleeting Hitchcockian presence), between the grind and the poet, the quiet worried scholarship-boy who is destroyed and the 'checkered and striking personality' who runs away and lives to fight another day. Unalerted to this parallel, we should read *Beneath the Wheel* as simply a straightforward warning, touching and telling, against the evils of subjecting a boy to the academic grindstone at a time when he should be giving himself up to the beneficent sway of nature. The slight smell of metaphysical *Lederhosen* which pervades Hesse's work is rather less metaphysical than usual here and more physical. And none the worse for that—but why must Hans die? Surely not that Hermann may live?

It is not so much that Hesse dramatises or even popularises ideas as that he takes the stiffening out of them, sandpapers the sharper edges away, and hands them over to his readers to play with as they will. A highly cultivated person, he is the ideal second-order writer for the sort of serious-minded reader desirous to believe that he is grappling successfully with intellectual and artistic profundities of the first order. Best among his books, I would say, are *Steppenwolf* for queer fun and mystification and some shrewd comments on the bourgeoisie, and *Narcissus and Goldmund* for a fairminded (if not consciously intended) assessment of some of those polar opposites so interesting to us all (for who wants to feel himself underprivileged in the matter of souls?) and so obsessively fascinating to the romantic German mind. (1968)

SEEKING THE UNDISCOVERABLE

HERMANN BROCH'S enormous trilogy, *The Sleep-walkers* (1932), begins with old Herr von Pasenow, an excellent short sketch of character both physical and moral, and it ends with a long and rebarbatively abstract epilogue, the tenth instalment of a sequence of similar disquisitions on the 'Disintegration of Values' which sadly weaken the impact and hardly clarify the significance of the third part of the trilogy. *The Death of Virgil* (1945) constitutes a marked advance, or prolongation, in the direction indicated by the philosophising parts of the earlier work, though with this difference: that the reflections of the dying Virgil, while equally abstract, are largely unargued, they proceed less by logic than by what alas is called 'poetry', sometimes reminding us of *Thus Spake Zarathustra*, but rarefied, diluted and inflated, lacking in pointedness and in Nietzsche's dubious yet undoubted excitement.

Formally *The Death of Virgil* has been described more or less aptly by a number of admirers. Thus Hannah Arendt calls it an 'uninterrupted flow of lyrical speculation leading through the last twenty-four hours of the dying poet'. (H. M. Waidson estimates it at eighteen hours: to me both estimates *seem* highly conservative.) And George Steiner has said that the book 'represents the only genuine technical advance that fiction has made since *Ulysses*'. But few critics, so far as I know, have attempted to ascertain the success, as distinct from the intention, of the novel, and the usefulness, rather than the nature, of the technique. Two questions are provoked by the descriptions I have just quoted. Could it be that what a flow of lyrical speculation needs is precisely to be interrupted from time to time by the unlyrical and the known? And can a technical advance be 'genuinely' an advance if its prime effect is to produce unreadability? But then, the argument of *The Death of Virgil* is so abstract, assertive yet evasive, so highflown and yet so narrow in compass, that one hardly feels inclined to study it with the closeness that a critical appraisal would require. It is safer to exclaim, 'A great European novel!' and leave it at that. Which, fair enough, will serve to warn off the great majority of potential readers.

In form *The Death of Virgil* consists of almost continuous interior monologue, in sentences so long that their beginnings are forgotten before their ends are known, varied by a conversation between Virgil and Augustus of a length and earnestness which no sick man could possibly sustain, and a scene with Virgil's friends which, modest as it is, seems to me much nearer the sublime than anything else in the work. The book's speculative profundity can be indicated by a few quotations. 'What we seek is submerged and we should not seek it as it mocks us by its very undiscoverability.' Or 'Only he who is able to perceive death is also able to perceive life'. Broch's prose poetry is rather similar to Rilke's poetry deprived of most of what makes it poetry, or occasionally reminiscent of the more sanctimonious or portentous lines of *Four Quartets*. '. . . the evil of man's imprisoned soul, the soul for which every liberation turns into a new imprisonment, again and again.' The style is heavily paradoxical. 'Shadowily projecting the formless into form, and floating between non-being and being . . .' ' . . .this always known yet never known goal.' It is the old Germanic taste for picturing the unpictureable, defining the indefinable, uttering the unutterable. . . . For one who aims at 'the word beyond speech', Broch displays a most remarkable fluency in the written word.

Even the highest and most subtle speculation must have something to speculate about. The main subject for speculation here, the meatiest bone in a voluminous soup of words, is art, beauty or poetry—and those grave doubts about the propriety of art which loom large in German writing, from Goethe and before to Thomas Mann and after. Striving 'to build up the imperishable from things that perish', art is 'pitiless toward human sorrow'. Beauty is cruelty, 'the growing cruelty of the unbridled game . . . the voluptuous, knowledge-disdaining pleasure of an earthly sham-infinity. . .'. The poet is 'unwilling to help', unable to help; 'shy of communion and locked in the prison of art', he depicts kings, heroes and fable-shepherds: but real human people, the men and women in the street whose curses Virgil hears from his sick-bed—these mean nothing to him. The poet therefore is a 'perjurer', he perjures reality. In itself the idea is certainly worthy of attention, but the argument spins in claustrophobic circles, for the most part swathed in language which you cannot get your fingers round, so that before long it comes to seem hardly more meaningful than (say) the assertion that coffee drinking is a cause of cancer. Is poetry really *that* bad? *How* bad is that bad? Are poets worse than mass-murderers? What poetry? Which poets? 'The concern of art was how to maintain equilibrium, the great equilibrium at the transported periphery, and its unspeakably floating and fugitive symbol, which never reflected the isolated content of things but only their interconnections, this being the only way in which the symbol fulfilled its function, since it was only through this interconnection that the contradictions of existence fell into a balance, in which alone the various contradictory trends of the human instincts were comprehended. . . .'

It might seem high irony indeed to read immediately thereafter that 'the grace-bearing saviour was one who has cast off from himself the language of beauty . . . he has pushed on to simple words . . . the simple language of spontaneous kindness, the language of spontaneous human virtue, the language of awakening'. This, perhaps, is Virgil's prefiguration of the language of Christ. The habitual language of *The Death of Virgil*—with all due respect to the author, who wrote the book while a refugee from Nazi Germany—is undeniably one of those Germanic languages which Günter Grass assaults in *Dog Years*: it is a way of almost not saying anything. Broch is obviously a conscious victim of this un-Christlike verbalism, and not a linguistic miscreant. His very diagnosis is symptomatic. Remembering Erich Heller's comment that Thomas Mann's *Doctor Faustus* is 'its own critique, and that in the most thoroughgoing manner imaginable,' we might cleverly propose that *The Death of Virgil* too is a thorough-going critique of itself. But then it will surely have to be admitted that the discrepancy between the massiveness of the critique and the slightness of what is being criticised is disconcertingly pronounced.

'Peasants are the real people,' says Virgil in one of his few undecorated statements. Poets aren't people at all: by striving to rise above, they fall below. And so Virgil desires to burn his *Aeneid*. Virgil is made to regret his poetry—and made to regret it in Broch's ineffable poetic prose. . . . Happily Caesar, to whom the work is dedicated, does not wait for the things that are his to be rendered unto him: he takes them. Augustus orders the manuscript to be carted off in a chest. What Broch thinks of this behaviour—collusion between art and the State? —it is impossible to say. And Virgil has no choice but to make his will and die. (1965)

PALE ORGANISMS

The Art of Vladimir Nabokov

VLADIMIR NABOKOV has written quite a lot about Vladimir Nabokov, and now Page Stegner has written about him too.[1] It must be said that Mr Stegner's approach is a good deal less sophisticated than Nabokov's. For one thing, in a slightly uneasy way Mr Stegner offers to *justify* Nabokov, to show that he possesses not only a brilliant style but also (though he 'tries to obfuscate that emotion by means of a brilliant style') a deeply compassionate nature. In a somewhat similar spirit Mr Stegner presents Humbert Humbert as a poor, compassion-worthy gentleman who was simply trying to recover his childhood by peeking at young girls. Unhappily he was seduced by Lolita, which spoilt everything. For Humbert, at least, though not for those readers 'who are able to transcend their socially conditioned response to sexual perversion'.

I wonder if anyone has written a book about Peter De Vries? Nabokov and De Vries are both considerable wits and word-boys, but whereas De Vries despairs of his fellow-beings without ceasing to love them altogether and finds the human condition pretty rough but still the only one we have, Nabokov loves memories, chiefly memories of his family, feels a large and fairly comprehensive distaste for the real, and seems to believe that 'words alone are certain good'. Nabokov, of course, is much more amenable to high-level discussion. The riddler always is, with the practically illimitable scope he offers for pattern-tracing, the pursuit of may-be allusions and might-be correspondences, which in the work of Nabokov amounts to a rich and welcome substitute for the old bone of symbolology that time and scholarly dentures have worn away. Unhappy about 'evaluation', an activity as tedious or as hazardous as grading examination scripts, our critics turn to free commentary

[1] *Escape into Aesthetics: The Art of Vladimir Nabokov*, by Page Stegner.

and explication, art grows increasingly aesthetic, criticism becomes a paper-chase, and never mind what is actually written
on the paper. . . .

I would say that *Pnin* is Nabokov's best book to date. Mr
Stegner opts for *Lolita*, but his section on *Pnin* is the most
warmly written, and I suspect that only his sense that *Pnin* is
insufficiently Nabokovian and that the admirer of Nabokov is in
honour bound to elevate *Lolita* has prevented him from coming
out in favour of *Pnin*. He goes as far as to acknowledge that

> perhaps because the composition is more straightforward and the
> controlling hand less apparent, *Pnin* is the most moving and real of
> Nabokov's characters. It seems as if both composer and solver,
> being less involved with intellectual gymnastics, are able to
> concentrate on the depiction and understanding of a truly *human*
> being and his redemptive response to the painfulness of exile.

'Most moving and real . . . a truly *human* being. . .' Yet '*Lolita*
is the greatest novel that Nabokov has yet written.' Few indeed
of Nabokov's fans have questioned the implications of his obsession with the superman hero, arrogant and (except where he
himself is concerned) callous, lording it over his natural in-
feriors. That the superman hero may be insane, or that eventually he slips up on a banana skin left in his way by normal,
mean, everyday reality makes little difference: we know where
Nabokov's sympathies lie. Perhaps he is a child of the times—
this would account for his ready acceptance at a number of
levels—but I incline to hope that he will not prove a father of
the future.

Chapters of *Speak, Memory* make this autobiographical work,
for me, a close rival to *Pnin*. In places memory speaks at too
great length, but more often with an hallucinatory and almost
suffocating density of minute detail before which one's own
memories of Nabokov's snobbery or peevishness, though only
a page or two earlier, fade almost to nothing. When he is
writing about someone or something he loves, he is irresistible;
when he is writing of someone or something he despises, he
can even manage to enlist one's sympathies, if only momentarily, for the object of his contempt. That Freudianism should

draw his scorn is understandable, since its elucidation of mysteries is so much less suave and subtle than Nabokov's propagation of them. Apparently his hatred of Communism is similarly simple and personal. He tells us—or rather he tells 'the particular idiot who, because he has lost a fortune in some crash, thinks he understands me'—that his old quarrel with the Soviets is 'wholly unrelated to any question of property'. It has to do with 'a hypertrophied sense of lost childhood, not sorrow for lost banknotes'.

Nabokov's childhood is not lost—or had to be lost that it might be found again, as it is in *Speak, Memory*, found with such seeming exactitude and depth and with such delicacy and tenderness. Sovietisation has been a professional blessing to Nabokov, providing him with the better part of his motivation as a writer, or with the motivation of the better part of his writing. The notification that his grievance has nothing to do with property (a curious little interlude altogether) was perhaps thought necessary in view of his having told us earlier that his family had 'a permanent staff of about fifty servants and no questions asked'. Perhaps it was time some questions were asked—even though the answers forthcoming were far from satisfactory. It may be an instance of his contempt for the reader's intelligence, or simply of his superb complacency, that having described the peasant girls outside his window, 'weeding a garden path on their hands and knees or gently raking the sun-mottled sand,' he adds in brackets, 'The happy days when they would be cleaning streets and digging canals for the State were still beyond the horizon.' We can feel vividly for Nabokov at the beginning of the 1920's, in exile (though in exile at Cambridge University), the son of a father who had been imprisoned under the Tsar, now obliged to contend with the 'pained surprise or polite sneers' of undergraduate socialists and armchair world-saviours. At the same time, his few references to the lower orders of his childhood ('a bedraggled hag who was gloating over a crimson-plumed hat on display at a milliner's') and his casual remark that he was not supposed to chat with the servants and didn't know how to, lead one to suspect that, while he loved and admired his father, it was not his father's liberalism which he admired.

Nabokov's curious self-righteousness displays itself rather comically when he is recalling his friendship with his cousin Yuri. At any rate I don't *think* this self-righteousness is a Nabokovian joke, for he is not given to joking in the presence of memory:

> The slums of sex were unknown to us. Had we ever happened to hear about two normal lads idiotically masturbating in each other's presence (as described so sympathetically, with all the smells, in modern American novels), the mere notion of such an act would have seemed to us as comic and impossible as sleeping with an amelus.[1]

The hit at modern American novels (not found in earlier versions of the autobiography) surely loses a good deal of its force when we recall that it comes from the novelist who penned the masturbatory epic of Humbert Humbert—though, granted, Humbert was not a lad and presumably not exactly normal either. But the forerunners of Lolita are charmingly evoked here. Colette, whom he met in Biarritz when he was ten, and attempted to run away with, getting as far as a cinema near the Casino. Polenka, 'always barefoot, rubbing her left instep against her right calf', whom he dreamt of but never spoke to, 'afraid of being revolted by her dirt-caked feet and stale-smelling clothes', for though not a servant herself, she was the daughter of the head coachman. And Tamara, who was 15 when he was 16, with whom he was forced to resort to cinemas and to museums until 'this or that hoary, blear-eyed, felt-soled attendant would grow suspicious and we would have to transfer our furtive frenzy elsewhere'.

> A light down, akin to that found on fruit of the almond group, lined her profile with a fine rim of radiance. . . . Her lovely neck was always bare, even in winter in St Petersburg, for she had managed to obtain permission to eschew the stifling collar of a Russian schoolgirl's uniform. . . . The rippling of her ready laughter, her rapid speech, the roll of her very uvular r, the tender, moist gleam on her lower eyelid . . .

[1] Amelus: a limbless foetus.

F

Tamara is a closer approach to Lolita, yet the story which Nabokov's memory tells is funny, and altogether endearing, and far removed from the (let's face it) thoroughly squalid Odyssey through the perils and discomforts of American motels of Humbert Humbert and his Dutch wife. Another attractive section (however unlepidopteristic the reader) is devoted to butterflies and their environment. The 'enthusiastic kitchen boy' who brought the young Vladimir a bagful of grasshoppers, sand, mushrooms and 'one battered Small White' is obviously the original of Fyodor's uncle's orderly in *The Gift*, one barely-spoken-to servant re-emerging as another. But then, you track Nabokov everywhere in his own snow—though I doubt there is much literary point in bringing out the bloodhounds every time.

One change from the earlier version of these memoirs, published in 1951 as *Conclusive Evidence*, is worth noting as an example of Nabokov's agility in mystery-mongering, and in that form of it which he most relishes since it concerns himself. Talking of Russian émigré writers, Nabokov stated in *Conclusive Evidence* that the one who interested him most was naturally Sirin, who belonged to his generation. 'Among the young writers produced in exile he turned out to be the only major one.' He remarked that 'Sirin's admirers made much, perhaps too much, of his unusual style, brilliant precision, functional imagery and that sort of thing,' and went on to mention by name 'the most haunting' of Sirin's novels— *Invitation to a Beheading* and *Luzhin's Defense*. 'V. Sirin' was Nabokov's pseudonym as a novelist writing in Russian, and since the publication of *Conclusive Evidence* the two novels in question have appeared in their English avatars. And so in *Speak, Memory*, in order to preserve the joke, such as it was, to save it from falling into utter ruin, Nabokov omits the reference to specific titles. And, as it seems out of modesty or out of faint-heartedness (weaknesses to which he is not normally prone), he has removed the sentence describing Sirin as the only major writer among the young émigrés and replaced it by something more acceptable: 'Among the young writers produced in exile he was the loneliest and most arrogant one.' Thus he not only salvages the joke but even improves it. The

Nabokov-reference in *Despair*, where Hermann mentions 'the well-known author of psychological novels ... very artificial, though not badly constructed', is sub-standard by comparison.

This sensitive and graceful life, though in *Speak, Memory* recorded so sensitively and gracefully, is not invariably as fascinating to read about as it must have been agreeable to live. The far-fetched language is at times doubtfully worth the carriage; these examples are all to be found on the same, strange page: fatidic, Joaneta Darc, praedormitary, *muscae volitantes*, hypnagogic, palpebral, photisms, *flou*. The love, the pathos and the entertainment come near to being outweighed by the haughty airs, the occasional archness and—an unexpected phenomenon in so sophisticated a person—the tinge of sanctimoniousness. You! *hypocrite lecteur!*—though not exactly Nabokov's fellow, and certainly not his brother.

The Waltz Invention (a play) and *The Eye* and *Despair* (novels) are translations (and in the first and last cases also revisions) of works by V. Sirin, originally written in 1938, 1930 and 1932 respectively. Each is now attended by a smug and somewhat aggressive foreword by V. Nabokov. *The Waltz Invention* is also accompanied by a blurb which is so grotesquely illiterate ('the frightening message is delivered with a shuttle to comedy, as indeed the ending is a happy one, because Salvator Waltz is not all there') as to seem to have been composed by Nabokov himself for the deeper damnation of the very baddest of his baddies. Waltz is in possession of 'an infernal machine' which will enable him to destroy the world; as indeed he is about to do when it transpires that the whole action is merely Waltz's dream while he waits to see the Minister of War. Waltz is loony—which makes hay of the publisher's claim for the work's prophetic qualities. Nabokov informs us that the play has no political 'message' and that he would not today have attempted to invent 'my poor Waltz'

> lest any part of me, even my shadow, even one shoulder of my shadow, might seem thereby to join in those 'peace' demonstrations conducted by old knaves and young fools, the only result of which is to give the necessary peace of mind to ruthless schemers in Tomsk or Atomsk ...

Yet he publishes the book today, even though there would seem to be reason for not publishing it beyond the author's squeamish horror of the sweaty caps and stinking breath of ban-the-bombers. It is a rather amateurish production, like a late specimen of a style of drama which failed to prosper in the 1920's.

The theme of *The Eye*, Nabokov tells us after uttering the prescriptive gibe at Freudians and the customary boast that his books are 'blessed by a total lack of social significance', is 'the pursuit of an investigation which leads the protagonist through a hell of mirrors and ends in the merging of twin images'— which sounds as if he has been studying his own interpreters. Though the story could be represented as *Lolita* in reverse, the supreme accomplishment of love residing in its non-accomplishment, it seems to me a light and fairly light-hearted piece of mild mystification. *Despair* is a more substantial and characteristic work, although its central deception falls short of Nabokov's usual elegance and involution. Its hero, Hermann, murders his double and changes clothes with him, partly in order to collect his own insurance, but chiefly (he informs us) out of sheer aesthetic delight, for the artistic achievement, the mastery of the thing. Hermann's carefully worked-out scheme fails because of a basic weakness: the reiterated resemblance between the two men exists only in Hermann's mind; for Hermann, it seems, is mad. But never mind, he gets a book out of it, and a highly gratifying fade-out. The novel contains a smattering of prime Nabokovianisms, such as 'Literature is Love', and 'a combination of decency and sentimentality is exactly equal to being a fool', and this account of the literary triangle:

> The pale organisms of literary heroes feeding under the author's supervision swell gradually with the reader's life-blood; so that the genius of a writer consists in giving them the faculty to adapt themselves to that—not very appetizing—food and thrive on it, sometimes for centuries.

Hermann's smugness is foreshadowed in the self-satisfaction of the foreword, where Nabokov instructs us that

Despair, in kinship with the rest of my books, has no social comment to make, no message to bring in its teeth. It does not uplift the spiritual organ of man, nor does it show humanity the right exit. It contains far fewer 'ideas' than do those rich vulgar novels that are acclaimed so hysterically in the short echo-walk between the ballyhoo and the hoot.

He continues, possibly because he feels he has been rather negative about the book:

Plain readers . . . will welcome its plain structure and pleasing plot . . . There are many entertaining conversations throughout the book, and the final scene with Felix in the wintry woods is of course great fun.

The 'final scene with Felix' is Felix's murder.

For Mr Stegner, as I have mentioned, *Lolita* is Nabokov's greatest novel. It is certainly, I would say, his most distasteful, arch, affected and perverse. It is also the novel which, in virtue of its story, provides the greatest scope for his macabre humour and his lepidopterist's analytic and classificatory skills. Linguistically it is his most 'brilliant' work, and if words didn't sometimes have meanings it could well be a great novel. As it is though, Nabokov is not going further than the 'conventional' great novelists whom he disdains; he is not going nearly so far. Some good, or some devilishly clever, if not always clean, fun is had by the way, but the way is short, it peters out in a maze of tracks which lead nowhere.

'While Humbert is a sexual pervert and a murderer, he is not a rapist; not a seducer of adolescent girls in dark alleys.' Agreed, Humbert tells his '*chère Dolorès*' that he wants to protect her from 'all the horrors that happen to little girls in coal sheds and alley ways'; but since he takes Lolita against her will by threatening her with incarceration in a reformatory, morally (if one may be allowed to use that word just once) he is not strikingly superior to a rapist. Though he talks of Humbert's 'tragic flaw', Mr Stegner doesn't go as far as one (at least) of Nabokov's admirers, who finds Humbert not a sexual maniac but a poet, a poet in pursuit of unattainable beauty. True, that checks with the dictionary definition of 'nympholepsy'. True, 'we poets never kill', Humbert has remarked; he also remarks, 'You can count on a murderer for a fancy prose style'. Familiar as one is with the vagaries, or the perversities, of contemporary criticism, it is still hard to stifle a small gasp as one watches a critic (not Mr Stegner) exalting Humbert into a secular saint on one page and on the next savaging the Headmistress of Beardsley School for uttering clichés and mixed metaphors! Words speak louder than actions after all, it seems. Thus the nauseous language of gallantry (parody? But parody is a plea that soon wears thin): 'the whole wine-sweet event', 'hot, opalescent, thick tears that poets and lovers shed', 'the honey of a spasm' (cf. the brisk, ungallant language employed by Humbert after he has succeeded in attaining the attainable: 'a quick connection before dinner'). Thus Humbert's request that the reader should try 'to discern the doe in me, trembling in the forest of my own iniquity': a jewel fourteen words long, as long as you don't think of what is happening, of what it *means*. Nabokov has succeeded too well with Lolita, too horribly well with Humbert, for the one to serve as symbol of unattainable beauty and the other as symbol of the poet. Here (if there ever can be) there can be no escape into aesthetics.

And is Headmistress Pratt much more than an Aunt Sally, a sitting duck? Nabokov sets up grotesques and then knocks them down adroitly: to feel superior to Miss Pratt or to Lolita's mother is the reader's compensation for his awareness of the contempt in which Nabokov holds him. Humbert's 'disgust for the false front of the gum-chewing American teen-ager'—oh dear, one begins to see innuendoes everywhere!— 'makes any parent nod in agreement'. So says Mr Stegner. It is nice that the parents of teen-agers should find common ground with Humbert, whom otherwise they might have mistaken for 'a madman with a gross liking for the *fruit vert*'. As for the send-up of motels and roadside restaurants, is it utterly improper to wonder whether a man who takes a young and not notably willing girl to such places is really in a position to complain of the décor, the food or the noisy lavatories? As satire *Lolita* is scarcely more caustic than *A Modest Proposal* would be if it transpired that its sponsor indulged a taste for fricasseed infant.

Like other writers on Nabokov, Mr Stegner has splendid fun tracing cross-references, following up clues and elucidating riddles. Until, while he is attempting to sort out the self-propagating exegetical possibilities of *Pale Fire*, a hangover sets in. 'One wishes,' he says, at last he says,

> that critics like Mary McCarthy who find a significant 'moral truth' in *Pale Fire* would somehow demonstrate where they found it, and how, and what it is. It seems to me that in their lengthy explications of the riddles in the novel they fall into the same trap that Nabokov has perhaps fallen into—that is, thinking that form and style alone will bear the burden of greatness and that a novel is outstanding because its structure is fantastically complex.

Pale Fire differs from Nabokov's other novels, at any rate the most celebrated of them, only in the degree of its tricksiness. All too generally this author, rich in what is given to few writers and poor in what is given to most men, brings to mind Gulley Jimson's comment in *The Horse's Mouth*: '. . . like farting Annie Laurie through a keyhole. It may be clever but is it worth the trouble?' (1966)

Eros, the Rose and the Sore: Nabokov's New Novel

To speak of the Master less than rhapsodically is to incur the fury of the Nabokovites, a large and vocal and merciless tribe whose war cry is 'Euphemism is Beauty, Beauty is Truth, etc.'. The Nabokovites find nothing so shockingly immoral as morality, and contend that the admittedly 'vile desires' of Humbert Humbert are transfigured by the 'poetic expression' of them, and anyone who worries over what (to use an unpoetic expression) 'goes on' in books is guilty of that most ludicrous solecism, the confusion of art with life. Their neat though not new aesthetic is presumably approved by the Master, who is reported to have said that 'Great novels are above all great fairy tales. . . .'.

To venture reservations about the stature of *Ada* is especially dangerous since for his fans this long new novel[1] is likely to be the Master's apotheosis, his *Tristram Shandy* where *Lolita* was his *Sentimental Journey*. Others, though, may find it his *reductio ad taedium*. Or, let us rather say, find it a book which, though you cannot put it down, you will never take up again once you have put it down. Which could be said, *mutatis mutandis*, of the most ingenious and startling conundrum ever; there is nothing so dull as a cracked code.

Ada is *Lolita* with substantial differences, *Lolita* civilised and sweetened by the Memory of *Speak, Memory*, 'that long-drawn sunset shadow of one's personal truth'. While Ada is 12 when she begins her sex life, her initiator, Van is only 14½, and their love lasts from their nonage into their nonagenariage. This wards off any slight queasiness which might have affected those readers who were so underbred as to think Humbert something of a dirty old man. Moreover, since Ada and Van are really (though supposedly cousins) sister and brother, they cannot marry as they would wish. The question of the moralistic critic is met: society has doomed them to clandestinity, somewhat like Romeo and Juliet. Morality satisfied, the situation is seen to have its other and artistic advantages: clandestinity has its thrills, like consanguinity. Nicest-Incest, says one of the more meaningful anagrams. This adds spice, but I cannot see that it supplies the philosophical meatiness which some American reviewers have detected. The Master sensibly prefers puns to symbols and his exegetes must sometimes remind him of the cold, clammy calculus of the badly frayed Dr Freud or Froid, Sigmund of Signy-Mondieu-Mondieu, M.D., M.D.

No nicest, no incest; no propriety, no impropriety. If the reader has no moral feelings or discards them *qua* reader, then much of the matter of *Ada* will mean little to him: if you cannot be disgusted, you cannot be charmed or moved or amused. Nabokov seems to grant as much in the most potent of the book's reiterated anagrams: 'Eros, the rose and the sore'. And true, the secondary characters here are livelier (and less heartlessly, so to speak, manipulated) than those of *Lolita*, while the primary figures are distinctly more engaging (nothing to do

[1] *Ada Or Ardor: A Family Chronicle.*

with 'engazhay', Maestro!) than grubby Lolita and shabby Humbert. Ada is intelligent and educated (it makes a difference) and Van is a genius (jolly good too!). We note, however, that Van is endowed with some of the usual perks of the porn-broker's dream-hero, vast wealth, enormous virility and irresistibility—if Ada is often lacking, ardour never is—and the blessing of sterility too.

There is a mint of riddle-solving and parody-spotting to be enjoyed here, and along with the reconditely cunning and the mediumly demanding (like reversing the opening sentence of *Anna Karenina* to make the opening sentence of *Ada*), there is plenty of stuff to be reassuringly deciphered by the commoner sort of reader and keep him on his bottom. 'Note', a school notorious for homosexuality; 'Manitobogan', a town; 'the Burning Swine', a poet ('a pest on his anapest!'); 'distressibles', decibels; 'the Chateau de Byron (or "She Yawns Castle")'. And in similar spirit, 'bric-à-Braques', 'the sunglasses of much-sung lasses' and (oh!) 'the lassitude that comes from "lass",' and (the same fish freud in an inferior Joycepan) 'the Mondefroid bleakhouse horsepittle'.

Good clean pun, if over-hectic. Yet that the lovers do so endearingly enjoy loving doesn't preclude a deal of voyeuristic gloating on the narrator's part. At times *Ada* reads like a parody of high-class nineteenth-century pornography—and by the way what *is* the difference between pornography and parody of pornography, except that some people feel happier about the latter, rather like those old-time executioners in the service of the state who used to deflower their virgin clients before beheading them? The preliminary *frottage*, a Humbert-thing, is vulgar, and commonplace by now. A crude, laughable, un-Nabokovian, Japanese product made play some years back with rush-hour mashing by *densha no samurai*, or in translation 'Those who enjoy cramped private transports in crammed public ones'. The flesh is a little too much and too coyly with us, whether merely 'one clavicle' or 'one russet knee', a 'bed-warm splenius', a 'nipplet' (to nymphet as nipple is to nymph), 'salty epithelium', 'ivorine thighs and haunches', 'pale, voluptuous, impermissible skin', or a 'chub' 'dusted with copper'. In some quarters the writer who avails himself of the epithet 'rosy' in conjunction with 'flesh' and of the word 'catamite' (another favourite is 'fondle', often found in the combination 'fondled and fouled') is considered a revolutionary stylist, new and nonpareil: the Nabokovites seem to have read nothing outside their all-embracing and well-read Master. The section on the schoolboy's dream of gilded sin, the Villa Venus, a chain of sumptuous seraglios, is (I would have said) plain porn—or, rather, plainly ornate porn. And a short extract from the account of the childish couple's first coupling, with its mixture of gallantry and bluntness, ought to show that Nabokov's style belongs to an ancient tradition:

> . . . Ada went down on all fours to rearrange the lap robe and cushions. Native girl imitating rabbit. He groped for and cupped her hot little slew from behind, then frantically scrambled into a boy's sandcastle-moulding position; but she turned over, naïvely ready to embrace him the way Juliet is recommended to receive her Romeo . . . now her four limbs were frankly around him as if she had been love-making for years in all our dreams—but impatient young passion . . . did not survive the first few blind thrusts; it burst at the lips of the orchid . . .

'One hates to write about those matters, it all comes out so improper, aesthetically speaking, in written descriptions. . . .' But the real wrongness crops up when Ada and Van are separated. There is nothing subtle about the insistent leer, the obsessive insinuation, and the innuendo without end—and often of a childish or crude sort. It is childish to bring in a nurse called Tatiana solely that she may (she does nothing else) write Van 'a charming and melancholy letter'. It is crude to introduce a part-time model solely that the reader can be told, 'You have seen her fondling a virile lipstick in Fellata ads'. The Master even sinks to the gross likening of two brown couches stacked in an attic to copulating beetles. He cannot leave ill alone. Let us turn a deaf ear to the whispering velleities of waning moralities—but Nabokov really should have heeded that stern taskmartyr, that unbribable Sorryboss, the Law of Diminishing Returns.

I ought to add that there are some plausible dealings with

Space-Time and an element of science fiction or 'physics fiction'. *Ada* is set on the planet Antiterra, sibling of our Terra, in 'Amerussia', which enables Nabokov to stir gouts of Russian into his sophisticated linguisticated stew and entertain us with witty easy quasi-anachronisms. All this makes a rich fantasticated field for the Naboprofs, but is rightly peripheral (in my reading at any rate) to the ardours of Eros, the rose and the sore, and chiefly of service in aiding the Adaless days on their way. For fairness's sake I had better quote the judgment of an American reviewer that *Ada* is 'a culminating work, an act of accommodation that in the face of darkness asserts joy . . . a great work of art, a necessary book, radiant and rapturous', and further evidence that its author is a peer of Kafka, Proust and Joyce. To me it seems further evidence that great gifts can be put to small uses, a mountain of words give birth to a mousse. My own guess is that it will find its peers among the Curiosities of Literature, as a specimen of the same class as *Finnegans Wake*, but less thorough-going, less single-minded, less pure and less proud than that work. In the meantime it will sell millions. (1969)

DANCING THE POLKA

COMPARED with *Pornografia*, *Lolita* (to which Gombrowicz's novel bears an obvious if superficial resemblance) is a veritable Odyssey of action and subject-matter. *Pornografia* treats of two elderly gentlemen, visiting a country estate in Poland in 1943, who imagine and then encourage an erotic relationship between two teen-agers, (a boy) and (a girl). The narrator, Gombrowicz himself, promises to explain this use of brackets, but fails to do so; never mind, the reader is more likely to resent his arch dealings with quotation marks. The two gentlemen erect a painstaking and tremulous construction of speculation and exegesis around gestures and actions for which there are innocent and obvious explanations, thus achieving an exceptionally refined form of voyeurism in that what is being watched quite possibly does not exist.

'Why this disgraceful passion for spying on people?' the narrator asks himself, and later tells himself, 'I ought to find some other occupation, something more suitable, more serious!' —a sentiment which after a while the most patient and well-disposed reader is likely to echo. But still this minute epic of uncertainty goes on: is there, isn't there, something between the two youngsters? On one page they are feared to be completely indifferent to each other, which spells 'the ruin of all our dreams'; on another we are told of a 'warm idyll in spring', so refreshing after 'stifling, grey years of horror and exhaustion . . . during which I had almost forgotten what beauty was. During which I had smelt nothing but the rank stench of death.' This might seem to offer a clue. In a time of war, of absurdity, what can there be 'more serious' or 'more suitable' to do? When the narrator drives into the nearest town, he remarks casually that it had not changed, 'it was just as it had been . . . And yet something was missing—there were no Jews.' The air of disdainful remoteness from the large and vulgar events of contemporary history brings Nabokov to mind. When a Resistance leader shows up at the house, the narrator is unable to 'control a vague feeling of disgust for all this décor—action, Resistance, the leader, conspiracy—like a bad novel, a late incarnation of more or less insane childhood dreams . . . The nation and its romanticism constituted for me an undrinkable potion concocted to spite and anger me.' Like Nabokov, who can give the impression that the Russian Revolution was concocted expressly to spite him, Gombrowicz is an émigré writer.

But this game of incitement and panderism—for the elderly gentlemen are not content to wait passively for something to happen—hardly comprises a telling alternative to the grey game of war and patriotism and politics. The apologia, or diagnosis, when it comes, is not especially cogent or engaging:

> I only took part in life like a whipped and mangy cur . . . But when at that age we are offered the opportunity of toying with blossom, of entering youth even at the expense of depravity, and if it appears that ugliness can still be used and absorbed by beauty, well . . . A temptation sweeping aside all obstacles, insurmountable ! Enthusiasm, yes, what am I saying ? folly, stifling, but on the other hand . . . No, it was mad ! Quite unsuitable !

These heart-searchings resemble nothing so much as a parody of the pact with the Devil in Thomas Mann's *Doctor Faustus*.

The ambiguous apotheosis of youth and its freshness and beauty in contrast to the ugliness of age, the equivocal glorification of adolescence over adulthood—all this is only vaguely Humbertian. It is only vaguely anything. By the end of the book the girl's fiancé (a young man but not in his first youth) has been killed along with three other characters, happily not including the teen-agers, unhappily not including the two old men. The much anticipated and striven-for love-making has still not been arrived at.

One realises and admires Gombrowicz's sensitiveness and subtlety, but would like to know what he is being sensitive to and subtle about. *Pornografia* is a skilful composition of gossamer threads, and altogether different from the pronounced (if poeticised) physicality of *Lolita*. Noticing the superficial kinship

with Nabokov, a British reviewer has remarked that Gombrowicz festers less. True, gossamer doesn't fester. But this
seems a doubtful point of superiority in the present case, for if
a story of this sort doesn't fester, it is hard to see what it can do.
The oldsters are not sex maniacs, they are simply incomprehen-
sible, simply weirdies. It would seem a perverse complaint to
make at a time like the present, but one is tempted to reproach
the book with failing to live up to its title.

Gombrowicz's earlier novel, *Ferdydurke* (first published in
English in 1961, though first published in Warsaw as far back
as 1937), prompts the reflection that what is amiss with *Pornografia* is that it isn't fantastic enough and so is merely odd.
Ferdydurke is very nearly fantastic enough. The apparent pre-
occupations and theories of the later novel are already present
here, indeed are more overt from the start. 'If you yourself
don't think yourself mature, how can you expect anybody
else to?' And, 'at heart man depends on the picture of himself
formed in the minds of others, even if the others are half-wits'.
Thus, where the elderly gentlemen of *Pornografia* can only
watch and negotiate, the 30-year-old hero of *Ferdydurke* finds
he has actually turned into a 15-year-old schoolboy.

'The senior is always the creation of the junior . . . Are we
not fatally in love with youth?' And so we are treated to some
ludicrous instances of 'old age obsequiously toadying to ath-
letic youth'. We are also treated to the asexual brand of
voyeurism offered by the later book. But the affinity here is seen
to be with Sterne's *Tristram Shandy* rather than with Nabokov.
There is a comparable mingling of satire, more or less good-
natured observations on human nature, a measure of deliberate
and cheerful absurdity, and anecdotage for the sheer sake of
anecdotage. There is also a similar mystification (the brackets
in *Pornografia* are reminiscent of Sterne's black and marbled
pages beneath which many truths 'lie mystically hidden') and
the author displays a like habit of addressing the reader in
admonitory or encouraging or pseudo-explicatory style. 'So I
invite all those who wish to plunge still deeper and get a still
better idea of what it is all about to turn to the next page and
read my *Philimor Honeycombed with Childishness*, for its mysterious symbolism contains the answer to all tormenting questions.'

As Jerzy Peterkiewicz remarked recently in *Encounter*, Gombrowicz is a teaser: 'and literary teasers do sometimes irritate. They provoke the reader or the audience, but are surprised when the provocation works.'

Without knowing of the book's strange and sad publishing history and its suppression in Poland, I doubt whether one would have spotted its supposed (and premonitory) political relevance, though one perceives and appreciates its timeless and unlocalised mockery, as in the interchange with the headmaster:

'Would you like to see the teaching body?'

'With the greatest of pleasure,' Pimko replied. 'It is well known that nothing has a greater effect on the mind than the body. . . .'

and his description of his staff as 'the best brains in the capital . . . Not one of them has an idea of his own in his head. . . All the members of my staff are perfect pupils, and they teach nothing that they have not been taught.' The book's superiority to *Pornografia* consists in its density of anecdote and even (however 'unrealistic') of character—among other items there is a very funny bedroom scene involving an unusually large cast—and its greater willingness to be comic, grotesque, wild, fantastic. Frothier on the surface, it none the less impresses as a more substantial piece of work. Perhaps it doesn't make much more sense than *Pornografia*, but it certainly provides more amusement.

'What a bore is the everlasting question: What did you mean by *Ferdydurke*?' Gombrowicz has written in his *Diaries*. 'Come, come, be more sensuous, less cerebral, start dancing with the book instead of asking for meanings.' He is against interpretation, it would seem. And yet there are passages in *Ferdydurke* so shrill and insistent (and passages so repetitious and tedious) that they will scarcely be denied 'interpretation': what else could they be crying out like that for? Even so, you can dance with the book quite merrily for much of the time, whereas with *Pornografia* you won't stagger more than a few steps before tripping over your partner. (1966)

ALWAYS NEW PAINS

Günter Grass's *Local Anaesthetic*

THE line between what one most admires in Günter Grass's writing and what one most resents is a remarkably fine one —and, it sometimes seems, a mobile one. His set-pieces possess a Dickensian quality, but happily Dickens had not heard about motifs and symbols and other such-like devices for doubtfully expressing the perfectly expressible, whereas Grass, who is a bit of a pedagogue, has. There is something of Dürer, of Bruegel and of Bosch in Grass's make-up; there is also something of Mary McCarthy's Mr Converse, the creative writing teacher who went through his students' work 'putting in the symbols'. Looking back, you may find you remember most vividly some horrific-farcical scene which in the actual reading was spoilt for you by the author's persistent nudging.

The density of Grass's writing derives in part from his documentation—for instance, the naval expertise in *Cat and Mouse* and the faustball and ballet material in *Dog Years*— though at times this documentation appears to be posing as a sort of autonomous allegory. In the new novel, *Local Anaesthetic*,[1] there is a fair amount of technical information about dental methods through the ages, and about geology, and more than a fair amount (for its relevance is more dubious) about the manufacture of cement, 'a commercially produced dusty powder. It is made by milling a slurry of limestone or marl, and clay, by crushing and grinding calcined cement clinker, by flotation and spray-drying in a rotary kiln . . .'

Much of this is interesting in itself and some of it is entertainingly presented, such as the lecture on various ways of cooking a literal goose given to a class of prisoners of war, their features 'sharp-cut from undernourishment', by a former hotel chef who is later to become a famous TV chef. Even so, there is a distinct discrepancy between the space this information

[1] Translated by Ralph Manheim.

occupies in the novel and its significant contribution to the novel. Generally in Dickens, documentation—what a person does for a living, where he lives, his favourite food and drink—is properly indistinguishable from characterisation—what a person is. And there is less room for inoperative material in this relatively short novel than in the mammoth *Dog Years*. *Dog Years* was a notably energetic work: as in *The Tin Drum*, a lot was going on even if some of the activity remained enigmatic. By comparison—by comparison with other novels by Grass, for when all is said, he is one of the very few authors whose next novel one has no intention of missing—*Local Anaesthetic* is a little on the tired side. Admittedly, that is inherent in its theme: a wearied, worried bafflement, the apparent homelessness in the affluent state of passion and ideals, even their possible dangerousness. After all, an Economic Miracle isn't as hateful as a Master Race in arms.... If the citizens have their eyes glued to the idiot-box, then just remember the commandants of concentration camps who read Hölderlin or played Schubert sonatas. The plump ladies stuffing themselves with *Torte* in the *Konditoreien* along the Kurfürstendamm are not a pretty sight, but are they moral monsters? 'Freedom of choice and second helpings. That's what they mean by democracy,' says a thin-skinned student. But the unnamed dentist who is 'symbolically' the most important presence in the book says this:

> Every day I have to combat injury to teeth caused or exacerbated by excessive cake consumption, by sweets as such. Nevertheless I refuse to demand the abolition of Kirsch Torte and hard candy. I can counsel moderation, repair the damage if it's not too late, and warn against generalizations which give an illusion of great leaps forward but—ultimately—result in immobility.

Really Grass has been most courageous. He has turned from the meaty material of Nazism and post-war moral chaos to the stolidly triumphant bourgeoisie of today's Bonn and West Berlin, from 'de-demonizing' the Third Reich (if that was what he was up to, and personally I never found him that cosy) to Chancellor Kiesinger and the aforementioned undemonic Ku'damm cafés.... My God, it almost seems that, but for

G

the Americans misbehaving in Vietnam, we could all live at
ease with our consciences for the first time since . . . Grass's
subject here is essentially this: what does St George do when
the local dragon is 'relatively' not such a bad beast and the
villagers are not especially terrorised by it? Yet dragons are
dragons—and do we want St George to lay aside his sword
and let it rust?

At the beginning of *Cat and Mouse*, the narrator, Pilenz,
was suffering from toothache. Teeth featured far more pro-
minently in *Dog Years*: Amsel's thirty-two teeth which were
lost to the fists of the SA youths and then replaced by thirty-
two gold teeth became a sort of referentless symbol or quasi-
musical motif. One wondered rather about those teeth—a Jew
who only lost his *teeth*? But in this new novel the narrator's
tooth trouble is exactly right, and his 'setting', in a dentist's
chair, superbly apt. Not merely because

> there was never yet philosopher
> That could endure the toothache patiently,

and not only because 'this pain . . . affects me, shakes me and
lays me bare more than the photographed pain of this world,
which for all its enormity is abstract because it doesn't hit my
nerve', but also because whereas radical action has the effect of
knocking teeth out, the dentist's concern is to keep them in by
conservative measures.

The patient, Starusch, is a high-school teacher under protracted treatment for a 'congenital and therefore authentic'
chopper bite caused by prognathism, and he is now 40 years of
age. At 17, under the name of Störtebeker, he had been leader
of a juvenile gang operating in Danzig-West Prussia ('the so-
called Dusters, a somewhat mysterious gang' whose mascot
was a 3-year-old child, we were told in *Cat and Mouse*), 'a
character with eyes very close together' and responsible for the
desecration of church altars and possibly acts even more repre-
hensible or (considering the nature of the regime at the time)
enterprising. 'We were against everything and everybody.'
But that was 23 years ago. And 'a teacher is a reoriented teen-
age gang leader who—if you don't mind taking me as an

example—has felt no other pain than toothache, toothache, for weeks. . .'.

No doubt the present cannot be truly understood without some knowledge of the past. And Starusch's pedagogic present would be a little uneventful by itself. . . . But fortunately the dentist has TV installed in his surgery, and the patient can watch either the regular programme or else the moving shadows of his own more exciting past, though whether real or imagined is hard to say. For Grass's old deliberate uncertainty—perhaps it happened like this, but maybe it happened like that—is present here too, though (I found) less irritating than in *Cat and Mouse*, while less rewarding than in the mystery of Matern (was he a Nazi, or an anti-fascist, or both?) in *Dog Years*.

Starusch has pedagogic pains as well as dental ones, and they are chiefly provoked by his favourite pupil, Scherbaum, an engaging young man who ought to go far. The question at the moment is how to prevent him from going too far. Starusch hopes to channel his pupil's idealistic ardour into the editorship of a run-down students' newspaper: in *Dots and Dashes* Scherbaum can agitate for limited smoking rights in school (though himself a non-smoker), maybe also fight for such other student demands as 'the abolition of religious instruction and the introduction of regular courses in philosophy and sociology'. But Scherbaum plans to make people understand what napalm is like by dousing his pet dachshund, Max, with gasoline and setting fire to the animal in full view of the *Kuchen*-eating Kiesinger-voting ladies in Kempinski's on the Ku'damm. (It looks as though 'K' is the magic-thematic letter here, perhaps in ironic allusion to the Nazi conception of the role of the female, '*Kinder, Küche, Kirche*'.)

This event—or, as it turns out, non-happening—is central to the novel, and again one appreciates the justness of it. It is not solely an ingenious product of Grass's black mischievousness, and the project has more point than could be seen in Matern's poisoning of Harras, father of Hitler's favourite dog, in *Dog Years*. The burning is intended as 'enlightenment by demonstration': Scherbaum would be quite ready to burn himself instead of his pet except that, Berliners being what they

are, only a dog can secure the desired effect. (There follow
statistics on dogs and dog-owners in West Berlin.) Indeed,

> Nowadays you could crucify Christ and raise the cross on
> Kurfürstendamm, let's say on the corner of Joachimsthaler, at the
> rush hour, the people will look on, they'll take pictures if they've
> got their gadgets on them, they'll push if they can't see, and be
> happy in the front rows because of the extra-special thrill; but if
> they see somebody burning a dog, burning a dog in Berlin, they'll
> hit him and go on hitting him until there's not a quiver left in him,
> and then they'll hit him some more.

We only regret that Grass should hammer away at the point,
hammering it home—and nearly to death—in an unposted
letter to a Berlin senator and in the narrator's speculations as to
whether statistics on canine losses in Vietnam mightn't stir the
population of Berlin more deeply than a human body count.
Starusch's attempts to dissuade his pupil from dog-burning
discredit him further among the revolutionary young whom
he is supposed to be teaching. His arguments are typically
'over-thirty' in nature, the self-extenuation of a has-been, a
potential cake-eater (once his teeth have been seen to), and
Scherbaum's girl-friend, Vero, reminds her co-radical that 'Mao
warns us against the motley intellectuals'. (Of what, though, is
Vero a True Image? A slogan-chanting front-line demonstrator,
but also a cake-eater on occasion, a collector of stuffed dogs
and 'artsy-craftsy knicknacks', and, Grass implies, perhaps moti-
vated by her adenoids, perhaps in need of one of those old
Germanic tranquillisers, *Kinder*, or at any rate the means
thereto. . . .)
In the end Max is spared. On the way to this non-climax
Grass treats us to some characteristic fun. Should Starusch
break his pupil's left arm and so incapacitate him? Should he
report him to the police? (Oh no, an ex-gang leader can't do
that!) What about burning Vero's stuffed dogs instead? (The
symbol of a symbol . . . .) Wouldn't it be better if Scherbaum
wrote The Ballad of Max the Dachshund, 'folk-naïve but hard-
hitting' and maybe a bit Brechtian? Should Starusch persuade
Scherbaum to let him undertake the burning (and get lynched)

while pupil and girl-friend hand out explanatory leaflets—in which case Starusch can procure a covered bitch and at the last moment 'find out' that it is an expectant mother and be released from his promise? Should he, with the assistance of Scherbaum's parents, poison Max in advance? Will the dentist, who is now treating pupil as well as teacher, provide Scherbaum with an injection for anaesthetizing poor Max? A sort of pseudo-climax is reached when, outside Kempinski's on a trial run, Starusch lists the ingredients of Schwarzwald Kirsch Torte and his sensitive pupil vomits violently, thus discomfiting some few of the cake-eating clientele. 'I'm not supposed to throw up,' Scherbaum complains, 'they are, when Max burns.'

Why does Scherbaum relinquish his project? 'He's given it up at your expense,' the dentist tells Starusch. 'Don't let it bother you. He says he wouldn't want to be like you, peddling the feats of a seventeen-year-old when he's forty.' By this time the dentist has become something of a father-figure for the teacher, to be teased a little, to be resented quite a lot, but to be taken seriously. . . . The reader may think it more likely that Scherbaum didn't burn his dog because he was fond of it, because burning is painful, because he isn't really a man of violence—or because the moderate, alleviatory counsels of the dentist have prevailed.

'Prevention's the cure!' The evolution of modern dental techniques has been a gradual process, and is undeniably a case of progress. The dentist refers his patient to old paintings of tooth-breaking by tongs, just as the teacher later shows his pupil slides of the burning of witches and heretics, of Dresden and Nagasaki, of the self-immolation of a Vietnamese nun. The dentist does not yank teeth out by violence, he seeks to repair them, to build them up, under anaesthetic if necessary. From time to time Starusch laments the brave days of his youth and his lost ideals: 'How is the gold become dim!' (Unlike the gold of Amsel's new teeth.) But in his Lamentations, Jeremiah continues thus: 'The young children ask bread, and no man breaketh it unto them'. There is no lack of bread in West Berlin, and if there were, then they could eat cake. Cake brings us back to the dentist's chair, and the blessings of anaesthetics and tranquillisers. . . . When, in a rebellious access of youthfulness, Starusch starts talking about a clean sweep and 'the transvaluation of all values', the dentist tells him that unless he abjures violence he will find that his jaw is being treated without benefit of anaesthetic. 'I retract.'

As for Vero, her boy-friend tells us that 'she reads Mao like my mother reads Rilke', a scathing comment—and the narrator tells us that later she marries a Canadian linguist. As for Scherbaum, he finds he has to compromise on what he prints in *Dots and Dashes* (cracks about Starusch and his engagement to a colleague are in, cracks about Kiesinger are out)—and he goes on to study medicine, another gradual and alleviatory art. As for Starusch himself, an abscess forms and he has to have the porcelain bridge sawn through. *'Immer neue Schmerzen'*— always new pains.

We don't need these concluding words to persuade us that Grass has not sold out to the comforts of comfort, the complacency of middle age, the ethos of 'I'm all right, Johann,' the convenient silence of the mouth-stopped cake-eaters. And, *pace Time Magazine*, I see no evidence here that he believes in 'the apparently helpless and surely tragic bankruptcy of liberalism'. He has simply noticed that clean sweeps leave a lot of room for more dirt, that revolution exacts a very high price for its problematical benefits. Starusch, after speaking of his past, says, 'Even though I survived them, those times made me what I am. I adapted myself. I developed compromise into a way of life. I clutched at reason. And so a radical gang leader became a moderate schoolteacher who in spite of everything regards himself as progressive.' By its very nature *Local Anaesthetic* is not the most exciting of Grass's novels, it is rather heavy-handed and repetitive and at times wastefully mystifying, but I would say it is certainly his most conscientious so far. (1970)

II

BEAUTIFUL CONTRADICTIONS

Shakespeare in Europe

THE coup against the discussion of Shakespeare's plays in terms of characters could well have been headed by teachers who were fed up with hearing students expatiating vulgarly, priggishly, facetiously or solemnly, on the dilatoriness of Hamlet, the lunes of Leontes, the senility of Lear or the imbecility of Desdemona (why didn't she sit down quietly with her husband and thrash things out?). . . . Then occurred the strategic retreat into the ivory citadels of symbolism, the promotion of the-play-as-a-whole, an excellent idea which soon came to mean *Hamlet* without the Prince and *Lear* without the King.

Now teachers must surely be fed up with hearing, vulgarly, priggishly, facetiously, solemnly, about the inversion of the natural order, about remorse, reconciliation, rebirth, restoration (as if these existed in a world without people and without human motivation), about images (as if these were simultaneously objects of barter and means of barter). . . . The revolution opened the way to a new cunningness, for as Bjørnstjerne Bjørnson remarked in 1865, 'clever criticism is the easiest of all forms of criticism', and the new formulae were even more amenable than the old speculations. Students ended up with something nice and clean, a metaphor drawn from metaphors, perhaps the 'enhancement' of the human into the mythological —itself an example, one might have thought, of the inversion of the natural order. No doubt the revolution reduced one pervasive sort of sentimentality, but at the cost of encouraging a rather trivial objectivity, even a coolness towards the subject-matter which in places evinces itself today as a systematic 'downgrading' of Shakespeare. His simpleness—a purveyor of commonplace ethics, a voice of the establishment, a primitive political scientist, a re-teller of myths and fairy tales—makes us, who expose him, subtle.

Vulgarity, etc., one can only deplore and seek to alleviate in the classroom as elsewhere, for the millennium is still far away. It may be that one means of alleviation is to look less patronisingly at older native views of Shakespeare—Johnson and Coleridge, for instance, should be read for what they say about him, not only for what they tell us about themselves—and also at views removed in space. Oswald LeWinter's well-edited compilation helps us in the latter respect.[1] And to pick a subject unportentous in itself but interesting in implication, we might look at Lessing, *c.* 1767, on ghosts. Since antiquity believed in ghosts, it was proper for antique poets to avail themselves of that belief. But can a modern poet, in an enlightened age, claim the licence for himself? Certainly not, not even if he sets his story in ancient times, for he will render himself incredible. Yet this abstention may result in severe artistic deprivation, so let us back-track a little. 'We no longer believe in ghosts? Who says so? Or, rather, what does that mean?' Deeper consideration suggests that the seeds of possible belief lie in us all—at least in those of us for whom writers write— and so the ball is back in the writer's court. In the end, Shakespeare can introduce ghosts—'his ghost in *Hamlet* makes our hairs stand on end, whether they cover a believing or an unbelieving brain'—but Voltaire had better not.

Goethe wrote that while the eye, 'the most facile of our organs of receptivity', may be thought of as the clearest of the senses, yet 'the inner sense is still clearer, and to it by means of words belongs the most sensitive and clear receptivity'. There is no true substitute for that inner sense or for the words which activate it: this is why the poems of Owen and Rosenberg still convey the experience of trench war more cogently, more enduringly, than the most powerful documentary film. If Goethe is arguing against stage representation, what of it? I think the contention that after all Shakespeare did write for the theatre counts for little alongside the fact that one can read him with such profit in the study: the latter is a sign of his distinction rather than our shortsightedness. Goethe himself preferred to 'sit with closed eyes and hear a naturally expressive voice recite, not declaim, a play of Shakespeare's', but in these

[1] *Shakespeare in Europe*, edited by Oswald LeWinter.

days such a *modus operandi* would be as difficult to procure as a reasonably undestructive stage performance.

Both Tieck and Chateaubriand, German and French, find themselves unable to admire the celebrated 'To be, or not to be', because it contradicts what is known of Hamlet's situation or experience or character. Indeed Tieck feels obliged to rescue the passage by means of a lengthy and unconvincing re-interpretation of its purport, a labour which he could have saved himself by attending more closely to what he himself says later about the 'mixture of heterogeneous ingredients' in Hamlet, something 'which we generally find in real life only in a much smaller measure . . . these beautiful contradictions from which nearly every gifted individual suffers to a greater or lesser degree'. This brings us to what is of paramount interest in Mr LeWinter's anthology. Shakespeare is so often re-proached in the name of realism with being insufficiently logical or consistent in his characterisation, and I don't think it will help to jettison the canon of realism for the sake of some putatively 'higher' reality, since to do so merely reduces Shakespeare's significance. The truth is that in this very trait, this weakness in logic or failure of consistency, he is being exquisitely realistic. I am not proposing that man is naturally irrational, only that 'irrationality' normally has its reasons, and if Shakespeare is worth reading, as distinct from gawking at, then he is worth reading thoughtfully. Despite grim memories of that fairly recent orgy of character interpretation, we cannot now be content (in Madariaga's words) with a Shakespeare 'who *depicted* characters without bothering as to their moti-vations', nor need we be. Associated with the complaint about defective realism is the critical propensity for a too easy sitting in judgment on such mixed characters as Antony and Cleopatra. Having examined this phenomenon elsewhere, I shall only remark that the desire for formulatable simplicities, though comprehensible, reminds me of a tick-the-right-answer question I stumbled on in Thailand: 'Moll Flanders is (*a*) a good woman (*b*) a bad woman.'

Mr LeWinter's Europeans are frequently perceptive in these matters. Talking of prophecy, madness, dreams, ghosts and fairies, Goethe asserts firmly that Shakespeare is 'naturalistic'

rather than 'romantic' and that 'the interests which vitalise
Shakespeare's great genius are interests which centre in this
world', the natural world and not the supernatural or preternatural. Croce comments that Shakespeare 'knows neither perfect saints, nor perfect sinners, for he feels the struggle at the
heart of reality as necessity, not as accident, artifice, or caprice'.
He adds that in this matter of justice the poet's 'indulgence' is a
lofty one, since 'his discernment of good and evil was acute',
and not the false indulgence which cancels or blurs the boun-
daries between virtue and vice. In like spirit Romain Rolland,
writing during the First World War, notes that even 'the vile
Edmund' is allowed some nobility at the last, and in this he
sees the 'human tenderness' and the 'blotting out of rancour'
which, as he rightly says, distinguish Shakespeare most from
the other dramatic works of his time.

Drawing a contrast between Molière's miser and hypocrite
and Shakespeare's Shylock and Angelo, Pushkin speaks of
Shakespeare's 'variegated and multiple characters', so far removed from the 'humours' caricatures with whom, such is
our insufficient faith in poetry's penetrative and flexible move-
ments, they are still apt to be confused. And Grillparzer points
out that 'Shakespeare's truth is a truth of impression and not of
analysis . . . It is reality that confronts us': not a new thought
but one which needs to be thought about anew from time to
time. Such is the force of that 'impression' that the critic can
and should hardly forbear from analysing, in which case he
must seek to render the analysis in some sense worthy of the
impression, and this he will only do by taking into lively
account that variegation and multiplicity. Finally, Jean-Louis
Barrault stands the simplification theory on its head, remarking
that Shakespeare 'gives his art the apparent confusion and complexity of Nature'. Surely this is what we really prize him, pre-
eminently, for: the real, legitimate and required, complexity
of his work, involving as it must do an apparent confusion, and
not for the confirmation of some banal moral/metaphysical/
mythological/anthropological theorem. At the best the commentator is bound to simplify, to systematise, but he can at least
show respect for his *raison d'être* by maintaining a guard against
gross over-simplification and a too schematic systematisation.

Most of the passages in Mr LeWinter's admirable addition to the Penguin Shakespeare Library possess interest of some sort, if not always direct illumination. Victor Hugo and Heine, French and German, may set us thinking how restrained and even laconic, after all, are the most excitable of our English romantic critics and the most effusive of our heroine-worshippers. Manzoni on Shakespeare *versus* the Unities sounds like Samuel Johnson, and Stendhal, in an amusing dialogue between the Academician and the Romantic, even more:

> You concede, then, that the spectator can *imagine* a more considerable period of time is passing than that during which he is sitting in the theatre. But, tell me, will he be able to imagine that the passing time is a period double the real time, treble, quadruple, or one hundred times more considerable? Where shall we stop?

Hofmannsthal mounts an exhibition of rarefied intellect which must appal us lowfalutin Englishmen, while Taine worries over Shakespeare's most immoderate violation of language (like Donne's heart, it thrives on battery and rape!), deplores the amount of crime and passion in evidence, but allows that somehow or other Shakespeare is 'the most marvellous of all creators of souls'. Protesting against a particular rendering of Shylock in 1910 as 'dislocated, trivial, and nightmarish', Ortega y Gasset launches into a feeling sermon against anti-Semitism.

Grillparzer is quite unable to stomach the 'absurd assumption' underlying *Measure for Measure*: 'a law imparting punishment by death to everyone who has had physical contact with a woman is plausible only under some fairy-tale caliph in the *Thousand and One Nights*. Hence the entire work seems somewhat arbitrary.' Stranger laws or stranger over-ridings of the law were to be observed in his vicinity less than a hundred years after he wrote—it is never wholly safe, it would seem, to attack Shakespeare on the grounds of implausibility! But for Tolstoy English drama was made up of murders, executions, battles and puns, and Shakespeare was the prime villain for writing Shakespeare, with Goethe not far behind for selling Shakespeare to Europe. *Pace* Mr LeWinter, Tolstoy on Shakespeare is merely sad and boring, unless perhaps the desperate extremity of his ill will (as when he objects to Edgar's naming of devils because this character couldn't possibly have read Samuel Harsnett's *Declaration of Egregious Popish Impostures*) can be made to yield entertainment. Where many of these European writers, as the editor points out, were making apt use of Shakespeare as a sturdy weapon in the battle for artistic freedom, Tolstoy was misguidedly attempting to use him for the promotion of the contrary cause. (1970)

CAVAFY: POET-HISTORIAN

IN introducing Rae Dalven's *Complete Poems of C. P. Cavafy* in 1961, Auden remarked that a poem by Cavafy, whoever the translator, was at once recognisable as a poem by Cavafy. This he attributed to 'a tone of voice, a personal speech' characteristic of the Alexandrian-Greek poet. It is difficult to say very much more than that. Though my admiration for Cavafy has continued to rise ever since John Mavrogordato's important volume of translations came out in 1951, I have never found an adequate way of describing his peculiar attractiveness, or of analysing the relevance one senses, somewhat unexpectedly, in reading his poems set in the remote Panhellenic world. Cavafy himself died in 1933.

Yet there can hardly be a tone of voice divorced from subject matter, a personal speech without something being said. And in many of his best poems Cavafy is saying something true and moving about the stoicism and fortitude demanded of losers. Sometimes the situation he sketches has a humorous aspect. Thus, 'In a Township of Asia Minor':

> The news of the outcome of the naval battle, at Actium,
> was most certainly unexpected.
> But there is no need to compose a new address.
> Only the name needs to be changed. There, in the last
> lines, instead of 'Having liberated the Romans
> from the ruinous Octavius,
> that parody, as it were, of Caesar,'
> now we will put, 'Having liberated the Romans
> from the ruinous Antony.'
> The whole text fits in beautifully . . .[1]

With some adjustment to the terminology, this could describe public attitudes in a Vietnamese hamlet which has been held in

[1] All quotations are from Rae Dalven's translations.

turn by the South Vietnamese and the Vietcong. An attitude of prudential adaptation to forces which cannot be met head-on— though in the case of the Vietnamese villagers, so much nearer the storm centre, the humour would be somewhat less in evidence, the desperation more.

The Alexandrian underdogs did occasionally have their day out, perhaps enjoying the spectacle of Cleopatra's children being made kings, among them Caesarion, 'all grace and beauty':

> they grew enthusiastic, and they cheered
> in Greek and in Egyptian and some in Hebrew,
> enchanted by the gorgeous spectacle—
> knowing full well the worth of all these,
> what hollow words these kingships were.

A pathetic sequel is the poem 'Caesarion', in which Cavafy evokes the figure of the young man, another if slightly more glamorous victim of power politics, about whom history says little:

> in vanquished Alexandria,
> wan and weary, idealistic in your sorrow,
> still hoping that they would pity you,
> the wicked—who murmured 'Too many Caesars.'

Also 'relevant', also (and not exclusively) Asian, is a poem about political reformers. Things are not going as well as they might, so experts are called in; but

> the handicap and the hardship
> are that these Reformers make
> a big story out of everything . . .
>   they inquire and investigate,
> and immediately they think of radical reforms,
> with the request that they be executed without delay.

'They also have a bent for sacrifices,' to be made by other people, and when at last they have finished their work and left, 'carrying off their rightful salary', you may feel that after all it is preferable to go on as before. More obliquely pertinent is 'The First Step', in which the young Eumenes complains that after two years of labour he has only completed one idyll. Theocritus reproves him: he should feel proud that he has advanced so far, for it means

> you must rightfully be a citizen
> of the city of ideas.
> And in that city it is hard
> and rare to be naturalised.
> In her market place you find Lawmakers
> whom no adventurer can dupe.

Besides what Theocritus is saying about the privilege of creativity, we receive—largely through the word 'naturalised' with its load of associations—a sense of contemporary political engineering, of our own world of new and old states, our age of passports, and the helpless victims of nationalism and nationality, the little people who lack the adventurer's skill in duping lawmakers and immigration officials.

One of the finest of Cavafy's stoic poems is 'Thermopylae', about those who keep faith with what they believe and tell the truth 'without rancour for those who lie', even though they foresee—'and many do foresee'—

> that Ephialtes will finally appear,
> and in the end the Medes will go through.

Another is 'The God Forsakes Antony', which is also adroitly generalised into speaking for all who see the failure of their work. Do not be fooled, Cavafy says, do not deceive yourself that your ears deceived you, but show yourself worthy of what you are losing, worthy of the success for which you strove unsuccessfully:

> approach the window with firm step,
> and listen with emotion, but not
> with the entreaties and complaints of the coward,
> as a last enjoyment listen to the sounds,

H

the exquisite instruments of the mystical troupe,
and bid her farewell, the Alexandria you are losing.

There is a dignity and a tenderness about these unrhetorical
exhortations to courage and fortitude which save them from
the faintest suggestion of the stiff upper lip or the hearty scout-
master. Yet they are equally free from self-indulgence, the
'firm step' is there as well as the 'emotion'. In other circumstances Destiny is seen wryly as an artist; two lovers are separated by brute necessity, 'the needs of a living', but their grief
is palliated, just a little, by the thought that Destiny has divided
them before Time could change them,

> so each for the other will remain forever as he had been,
> a handsome young man of twenty-four years.

Cavafy once said that while many poets were exclusively
poets, he was a poet-historian. In this case we must agree with
Sidney that 'the best of the historian is subject to the poet', for
whatever action the historian is bound to record, 'that may the
poet with his imitation make his own, beautifying it both for
further teaching and more delighting, as it pleaseth him'. The
young and vigorous Nero sleeps soundly on his ebony bed,
while his small household gods fall over one another in panic
as they recognise the iron footsteps of the Furies on the stairs.
A travelling salesman in Alexandria, 31 B.C., can't sell his
Brylcreem or Old Spice because of the inexplicable noise and
excitement, the music and the parades; finally someone in the
crowd

> hurls at him also the gigantic lie
> of the palace—that in Greece Antony is victorious.

At Delphi the priests are delighted with the gifts presented by
the envoys of the two rival Ptolemies, but sorely embarrassed
by the consideration that one party or the other must inevitably
be displeased by the oracle's verdict. While they are delibera-
ting, the envoys suddenly depart, happily leaving the gifts
behind. The envoys have heard, as the priests have not, that

'the oracle was pronounced in Rome; the division took place there'. It seems so casual, so easy to do, this historical-poetic miniature painting, yet very few people have done it with anything like Cavafy's neatness, lucidity and unemphatic force.

His poems on the subject of homosexual love form a much less interesting section of Cavafy's work, I think. It is true, as Auden said, that Cavafy is an exceptionally honest witness who 'neither bowdlerises nor glamorises nor giggles'. But for all their typical terseness these poems are repetitious where the 'historical' ones are not; and, not surprisingly when emotion is recollected in age's untranquillity, there is an element of gloating in the references to 'the ardour', 'the supreme pleasure', 'the delightful stored-up sensual emotion'. More business-like, certainly, are the poems in which the poet relates his physical pleasure to his art. Out in the street, the young men are uneasy, as if something about them must reveal what sort of bed they have just risen from:

> But how the life of the artist has gained.
> Tomorrow, the next day, years later, the vigorous verses
> will be composed that had their beginning here.

Auden felt it was all very well for the poet, who could exploit such experiences—but what would be the future of the artist's companion? One takes the point, yet it is only fair to remark that the protagonists are consenting and adult and moreover the possibilities of pain are not played down. Cavafy describes the fate of one handsome boy:

> Of course, no statue or painting was ever done of him;
> cast into the filthy old ironmonger's,
> quickly, by heavy labour,
> and by common debauchery, so wretched, he was destroyed.

The best of this group is 'He asked about the Quality', where the keen, economical, simple-seeming presentation of a small drama—a young man is drawn into a shabby shop by a glimpse of the assistant—reminds us of the historical pieces:

They kept on finding something to say about the merchandise—
but their only aim: the touching of their hands
over the handkerchiefs; the coming close
of their faces, by chance their lips;
a momentary contact of the limbs.

Furtive and fleet, so that the storekeeper
who sat in the rear would not notice anything.

That I have quoted copiously is further recognition that
Cavafy's charm, so hard to analyse, speaks best for itself, his
poems are the only description of themselves. The combination
of tenderness with irony, the cool confrontation of disaster,
the gift of nimbly enlarging a specific historical incident into
general applicability, give him the right to that touch of arrogance which he ascribes to 'A Byzantine Noble in Exile
Writing Verses':

Let the flippant call me flippant.
In serious matters I have always been
most diligent . . .
it is not at all peculiar that I amuse myself
composing sestets and octets . . .
and that I compose impeccable iambics,
such as—permit me to say—Constantinople's men of letters
    cannot compose.
This very accuracy, probably, is the cause of their censure.

(1970)

'THAT THE EXISTING
BE WELL INTERPRETED'

Hölderlin in English

I NOTICE that in 1942, in the rashness and ignorance of youth, I described Hölderlin as 'that rare thing, a genuinely philosophical poet'. In extenuation I might now plead that the occasion was a review of August Closs's *Hölderlin: Gedichte* (a pioneering selection in England, and effectively my introduction to the poet) and that I was about to contrast him with Rilke, then enormously fashionable, who as time passes seems to me ever less philosophical and even less genuine. Rilke's genius could slide so easily and unnoticed into legerdemain and bamboozlement, whereas there is always a careful honesty about Hölderlin, a quality which emerges touchingly in the poems of his madness as a scrupulous tentativeness. I might also plead that after all Hölderlin is discernibly a 'thinker' and no one would feel imperatively called upon to describe him as *not* a genuinely philosophical poet.

The trouble is, though, that to talk about his thought is to say surprisingly little about his poetry. You find you have thrown a whale to catch a sprat. Hölderlin's best English commentators are Michael Hamburger and J. B. Leishman, who have woven his writings generously into their commentaries, and E. L. Stahl, who by pursuing Hölderlin's symbolism has sought to elicit his 'poetic thought' rather than 'his thought as such'. The problem is of course not unique to Hölderlin. Yet very many poets can be discussed, however incompletely, in terms of their thought, their attitudes, their desiderations. Hölderlin is a rather extreme instance of those who cannot be so discussed even though on the face of it they would seem more than usually responsive to the procedure. So perfectly is 'what is said' subsumed in 'the way of saying', so immediately and completely coincident are statement, rhythm and tone, that almost—and this would be no more illuminating though perhaps it might be less misleading—one is tempted to rest content with a metrical analysis. Characteristic of Hölderlin's poetry is its continuousness: the way, let's say, the opening lines of a poem (and not necessarily a short one) are still sounding as one reaches the close. The term 'form' is ambiguous, to put it mildly, for we find it most energetically deployed in the case of poetry which possesses little apart from form, little else to compete for our attention. With Hölderlin subject-matter is *known* to be there, solidly present; you couldn't for a moment suspect that he was talking about nothing very much. Here perhaps the concept of form can have a positive meaning instead of an exculpatory function. One is certainly drawn, far more strongly than with (say) Goethe's *Römische Elegien*, into an awareness of formal qualities, of the shapeliness of the verse in the whole and at every point, of its almost tactile nature (the poet of the *Römische Elegien* tracing the rhythms of his hexameters on his mistress's back)—or, better, of a musical organisation which remains in the reader's mind after the words, and certainly after the thoughts, have faded. Hölderlin's is a poetry of distinctive acoustics—distinctively German to begin with, and then distinctively personal.

The best things that have been said about Hölderlin seem inadequate. H. L. Bradbrook speaks of 'simple felicity' and 'natural piety': the felicity only seems simple because it is so felicitous, while the second phrase suggests a bucolic goodiness more readily come across in Wordsworth than in the German poet. August Closs refers to the characteristic 'surging rhythm', which is apt, yet the movement ebbs as well as flows and at times is held magically frozen, a phenomenon intimated by Mr Hamburger's remarks about the poems' cadences, 'their peculiar dynamism, their peculiar stillness, brought about by the tension between a strict form and an impulse beating against it'.

Such poetry will be immensely difficult to translate, and would appear unamenable to what is called 'imitation'. In any case imitation strikes me as a highly dubious activity, of more use to the imitating poet (as a means of keeping his tools in trim and himself out of trouble) than to anyone else. Its products are customarily neither fish, flesh nor good red Loebian herring. Currently, imitation holds out considerable attractions

to poets who have no subject to hand (a not uncommon contemporary situation) but possess a well-developed style. The
imitated poet is plundered for his subject-matter, to which,
suitable adjustments having been made, the imitator applies
his own idiom. Mr Hamburger describes the practice rather
nicely as 'a kind of occupational therapy for poets partly or
temporarily disabled'.

If Mr Hamburger were not so active in other spheres, one
would think of the Englishing of Hölderlin as his life's work.
His first translations of the poet came out in 1943, a revised
and enlarged edition appeared in 1952, and in 1961 he published
a generous selection of prose versions in the Penguin Poets
series. Though a poet himself, Mr Hamburger doesn't make use
of the German poet to show off his own creative talents. He
has far too deep a respect for Hölderlin to be able to 'imitate'
him. His guiding principle (which he attributes amusingly to
'a residual puritanism') of keeping as close as possible to the
sense and the cadences of the original poems impresses me as
absolutely correct, both morally (if one may venture such a
judgment) and poetically. To say that it is correct poetically
is simply to acclaim the results of Mr Hamburger's policy, but
while it is true that nothing succeeds like success, it is even
nicer when a reasonably beautiful translation is also a reasonably
faithful one. Indeed Mr Hamburger's piety is one of the
qualities which fit him to translate precisely this poet. '*Seid nur
fromm* . . .' A respect for work achieved—an attitude as remote
from devotion to fashion as from self-aggrandising belittle-
ment—is quite a rare thing nowadays.

Or is it rather—one asks, looking at this new 600-page volume—a case of making a living out of Hölderlin?[1] No, as Mr
Hamburger has lived, so he has learnt. The new preface is
altogether admirable, and the new introduction (based on the
Penguin Poets introduction), which 'had to be kept as short as
possible', has made a virtue of necessity, for the introduction
to the 1952 selection took up a good third of the book. We now
have much more Hölderlin, including *The Archipelago*, the
whole of 'Reif sind, in Feuer getaucht . . .' (the third version

[1] *Friedrich Hölderlin: Poems and Fragments*, translated by Michael Hamburger.

of 'Mnemosyne'), and two dramatic fragments, *The Death of Empedocles*. In the course of revising Mr Hamburger has removed a few archaisms and smoothed out some clumsinesses. Mostly the changes are distinctly for the better: thus, 'Why did you keep / Away?' replaces 'Why have you been / Distant?' for '*Was bist du ferne / Geblieben?*' But not quite always: the lines in the 1952 version of *Patmos* ('*Wo aber Gefahr ist, wächst / Das Rettende auch*'),

> But where there is danger,
> The saving powers grow too

seem superior to the new rendering:

> But where danger threatens
> That which saves from it also grows.

And in 'My Possessions' Mr Hamburger has now made the storm, the heavenly powers, seem inappropriately baleful by turning Hölderlin's '*verzehrend*' and '*wechseln*' into 'They rend, destroy me'. His 1952 version is juster at this point, as is also the Penguin prose version, and the version given by J. B. Leishman in his *Selected Poems* of 1944 is the best of all.

Leishman was notoriously an eccentric translator, not (like the imitators) licentious in his treatment of the original but licentious in his dealings with the language he was translating into. At his worst, the effect is slightly ludicrous (except when you realise that none the less he is making a critical point about the original); at his best, he remains unsurpassed. Mr Hamburger renders the last four lines of the fourth stanza of *Menon's Lament for Diotima* thus:

> Desolate now is my house, and not only her they have taken,
>   No, but my own two eyes, myself have I lost, losing her,
> That is why, astray, like wandering phantoms I live now
>   *Must* live, I fear, and the rest long has seemed senseless to me.

Leishman gives:

> Ah, but desolate now my house! My eyes they have taken
> From me, and all that I was, oh, I have lost it with her!

Wherefore I gropingly wander, and here like the shadows in
                                                        Orcus
Linger, and all that remains long has seemed utterly vain.

If Leishman's introduction of Orcus is a liberty, then Mr
Hamburger's introduction of 'I fear' is not only a liberty but
also an inaptly pedantic touch. This is one of those passages
of Leishman which persist in a remembered music. Others
occur in his *Bread and Wine* (which, with 'wild'ring' for
'*Irrsaal*', provides an instance too of his vagaries)—a comparison
of the latter part of the seventh stanza shows that where
Leishman is gravely stoical Mr Hamburger is merely petulant
—and in his version of 'Hälfte des Lebens'. Mr Hamburger
translates this poem very well, but Leishman's version has an
extra sweetness, the singing sweetness of the original. Incidentally his third line is in a simple sense more accurate than
Mr Hamburger's as an equivalent for '*Und voll mit wilden
Rosen*'.

> With yellow pears the land
> And full of wild roses
> Hangs down into the lake,
> You lovely swans,
> And drunk with kisses
> You dip your heads
> Into the hallowed, the sober water.
>
> But oh, where shall I find
> When winter comes, the flowers, and where
> The sunshine
> And shade of the earth?
> The walls loom
> Speechless and cold, in the wind
> Weathercocks clatter.
>
> *(Hamburger)*
>
> With yellow pears leans over,
> And full of run-wild roses,
> The landi nto the lake,

You gracious swans,
And, drunk with kisses,
You dip your heads
In the sacredly-sober water.

Where shall I gather though,
When winter comes, the flowers, and where
The dappling shine
And shadow of earth?
The walls will stand
Speechless and cold, the wind-swung
Weather-vanes clatter.

                                        (*Leishman*)

But '*nicht alles will der Höchste zumal*', and whereas Leishman gave us a small (albeit excellent) selection, Mr Hamburger has now given us practically the whole canon. Apart from regretting that there should be no mention at all of Leishman's work here, one's only complaint might be that, though handsomely produced, the volume is of a rather austere presence, more appropriate to some genuinely philosophical author than to so warm-hearted a poet. (1967)

DIALECT AND ANALECT

A Life of Ezra Pound

NOEL STOCK'S *Life of Ezra Pound* belongs to the class of sobersided, factual, studiously researched biography which before long will be written by computers. It is not, that's to say, an example of 'creative' or 'critical' biography; and the impression it conveys of a living man comes largely from the aptly chosen quotations from Pound himself. The criticism in the literary sense seems to me thinner than need be and sometimes unconvincing, though whether the omission of the 'Ballad of the Goodly Fere' from Eliot's selection is a serious one, as Mr Stock maintains, or not, is a question of opinion. *De gustibus* . . . and where Pound is concerned it would appear, more bleakly than elsewhere, that one man's meat really is another's poison. To change tack, it probably isn't true that *man ist was er isst*, and so we do not need to know that the young Ezra drank eight lemonades on a day in June 1898—or that 'O heart o' me' was written in Gibraltar. But as an example of its kind, the book could only be seriously faulted, if at all, by someone prepared to work as hard as Mr Stock has done. Though unobtrusive, he is firm about Pound's most blatant eccentricities or ignorances, and if on some personal matters more momentous than lemonade-drinking he is almost wincingly reticent, at least this doesn't detract from the quiet dignity of his tone.

The book does throw light—though not, I think, new light —on the life and work of Pound. I found it sad reading, with an element of the life-enhancing none the less present: as if its subject were a much more sophisticated, much less majestic, and virtually unrepentant Lear. What it chiefly illuminates is the alarming discrepancy between theory and practice in Pound. There is no call to discuss again the central importance of Pound to the modern movement: he was its number-one turbine, we cannot imagine it without him. 'Half of the work that Pound did as a critic,' Eliot said, 'can be known only from the testimony of those who benefited from his conversation or correspondence': and the other, visible half is considerable enough. In his earlier years Pound was an excellent thinker *about poetry*. 'The perception of the intellect is given in the word, that of the emotions in the cadence. It is only, then, in the perfect rhythm joined to the perfect word that the twofold vision can be recorded.' His effort, he said, was 'toward using the living tongue'; if it were to mean much, poetry would have to live 'close to the thing' again. 'Go in fear of abstractions,' he advised; and, 'the natural object is always the *adequate* symbol.' It is hard to imagine any advice which would have been more timely than Pound's, or expressed with more clarity and less pretentiousness. And he could be acute about his own writing, too, as when he commented of 'Sestina: Altaforte' ('Damn it all! all this our South stinks peace') that while 'technically it is one of my best,' a poem about the stirring up of war 'could never be very important'. We may pause worriedly on the force given to the concept of 'technique' here, but must admire such perceptiveness in a context where that quality is rarely found.

But while Pound the critic and programmist was striding into the twentieth century, Pound the poet seems to have been stuck in the nineteenth, or in a nineteenth-century idea of the Middle Ages. His language veers between what sounds suspiciously like Wardour Street and what is uncomfortably close to Dowson and *fin de siècle*. By comparison, admittedly, the satirical pieces in their cool and relaxed English are all the more striking—but the price is an ominously high one. It is easier to respect early Yeats than early Pound, for the former, however out-dated, has its own genuineness and spontaneity, whereas there is a sense of perverse contrivance about the latter. In 1913 Yeats wrote that Pound 'has more sound principles than taste', which is just, I think, if by taste we mean that which guides the artist in the implementation of his principles. It must be added, for fairness, that Pound certainly had the 'taste' to recognise Yeats at once and for all as a great poet.

Mr Stock mentions a letter which Pound wrote to his father in 1903, marked by 'the use of foreign language, dialect, and strong English,' adding that 'Queer spellings and a great variety

of dialect voices gradually begin to creep into his letters: sometimes, it seems, for emphasis, but often as not for the sheer fun
of it.' It would be foolish to make too much of this, but it does
seem strange verbal behaviour for one who aimed at using 'the
living tongue' and bringing poetry 'close to the thing'. Words
were getting detached from things at an early stage in his
intellectual development, it might seem.

Given a tendency towards dialect, imitated or concocted, and
a taste for the archaic, Pound was an easy prey for the exotic,
remote in space as well as in time. Despite Eliot's claim that
Pound was the inventor of Chinese poetry for our time, I
think it was a disaster when in 1913 Pound acquired the literary
remains of Ernest Fenollosa, one of that still extant class of
talented amateurs devoted to the ancient and suspicious of the
modern of whom Lafcadio Hearn is probably the best known.
Pound found so many new toys to play with, free from com-
petition or restraint; and his tendency to believe that a thing
really was what Ezra said it was found a large new territory in
which to expand. I don't suppose it matters much, in itself, that
Li Po has been perpetuated as Rihaku (though the Chinese
might wonder why Pound handed over one of their very
greatest poets to the Japanese), or that in his version of the Nō
play, Suma Genji, titles of the books of The Tale of Genji have
been read as place names, or that there are at least two references
in Cathay to 'the River Kiang', although 'Kiang' means 'River'.
But since no literary advantage derives from these simple
misapprehensions, surely they could have been quietly cor-
rected by someone or other? This mixture of carelessness and
arrogance is the reverse side of Pound's energy and enterprise,
and it consorts ill with the insistence of himself and his followers
upon precision and clarity. (The carelessness is contagious; or
perhaps it is to make up for the Japanesification of Chinese Li
Po that Mr Stock has indexed references to the Japanese Nō
plays under 'Chinese plays'.) As one of the later Cantos puts it,

get a dictionary
and learn the meaning of words.

But more harmful was the ethico-political mythology he
erected out of Fenollosa's notebooks. The Chinese ideogram

became his god, the manifestation of indestructible clarity and
purity—yet Chinese is the trickiest of major languages—and
Confucius, a sort of rather superior Staff Tutor to a rather
superior sort of Civil Service, was his prophet. . . . The relevance of Confucius and his code to the China of his time (and
later) can be understood. Not so the relevance of either Confucius or ancient China to the Europe of Pound's time—
though of course one sees that the sage's antiseptic coolness
served to make more horrid the Shylockian greasiness of
modern usury. Yet such was the final extremity of Pound's
self-deception that in 1945 he could insist that the Chinese
Empire in its great periods provided the only working model
for the post-war world and his new versions of Confucius
the only solid foundation on which to build it. More amusingly,
one of the *Pisan Cantos* remarks in passing,

> you cannot yet buy one dish of Chinese food in all Italy
> hence the débâcle.

I believe that his unguided and undisciplined transactions
with Eastern literature and philosophy led swiftly to a widen-
ing of the gap between word and thing, between the daughters of earth and the sons of heaven, and to an encouraged confusion of the Poundian assertion with the objective reality. By
1937, Mr Stock says, he had become 'absorbed in a world of
make-believe over which he ruled according to laws of his
own devising'. And so he adopted Mussolini and Fascism as the
contemporary approximations to Confucius and the ideal
Chinese Empire. For Pound, Mr Stock writes, the high quality
of Mussolini's mind was demonstrated when the poet mentioned that he was trying to put his ideas in order and the Duce
asked, 'Why do you wish to put your ideas in order?' Pound
replied, 'For my poem'—the Cantos. Thus it was—to mention
a trivial phenomenon—that he could say of some minor
Western-inspired Japanese poets that 'Tokio takes over, where
Paris stopped'. Thus it was that we have the distressing sight of
a man of Pound's gifts producing his family tree to an English
anti-Semite who considered Mussolini a tool of the Jews, in
order to prove he had no Jewish blood in him. And thus it was

that he could write in 1935 that 'the mass of humanity in most of Abyssinia will be better under the Duce's rule, than under that of the Negus. The facts are ascertainable.' *The facts are ascertainable*—the phrase has the Staff Tutor's ring about it, but what happened to that dictionary and the meaning of words? Isn't this a case of that sickness Pound had described in *How to Read?*—'When the application of word to thing goes rotten, i.e. becomes slushy and inexact, or excessive or bloated, the whole machinery of social and of individual thought and order goes to pot.' In justice we must recall that at this very time Pound was busy resuscitating Vivaldi, besides (as always) producing fragments of fine poetry, notably when he was not seeking to thrust the present into the strait-jacket of a largely imaginary past.

So much remains that is admirable and inspiriting: the man's inexhaustible energy, his courage and fortitude, and of course his perceptiveness in many though not all literary matters. As for the other side of it, he paid the price (and rather more) for his follies and his bad advice—which is something that many are incapable of doing. Besides the grandiosity, there is something grand about Ezra Pound. (1970)

THIS OR SUCH WAS
POSSUM'S WAY

The Invisible Poet

The present, as we know, is an age of criticism. And much of the criticism is in its old age, the wisdom of prematurely aged dons thinking themselves new critics. Hugh Kenner planned a book on Eliot in 1949 but didn't write it. A book on Eliot in 1959, to be readable even, would need to be very different from what has gone before. Mr Kenner's—*The Invisible Poet*—often is. It contains pages which actually revive those innocent early days when one read Eliot for the first time, without benefit of commentary, since that 'whole smokeless industry' (as Mr Kenner calls it, perhaps mistaking his adjective) was in its infancy too.

Sometimes, though, *The Invisible Poet* is not different—only the same but more so. On the 'History' passage of 'Gerontion' this is certainly the case.

> Two sentences later something she gives too soon into weak hands is refused, and in consequence of the refusal there is a propagation: in this phantom world contraceptives and rejected opportunities usurp one another's negative functions.

As Mr Kenner slips smoothly and elegantly along the 'vaginal' corridors of the poem one finds oneself hoping desperately that Robert Graves will pop up and ask again why 'jew' is written with a small initial letter. Mr Kenner doesn't ask awkward questions. 'The Jew who was spawned in some estaminet of Antwerp,' he tells us, 'cannot but prolong into the present the reputation of another who was born in a different inn.' I should say that the jew could very well do no such thing. 'The sequence Antwerp, Brussels, London . . . remotely echoes Bethlehem, Jerusalem, Rome.' The bottom is a long way down, as was remarked in another connection, and remote can be

remote indeed. 'No written word moving without local context can shrug off the allusive weight of its own history,' states
Mr Kenner. But written words often move with a local context,
and the context in this case would seem to be quite continent
—firm enough, at any rate, to resist Mr Kenner's attempts to
shrug its weight off.

The sexegesis continues with 'the circuit of the shuddering
Bear'. Reminding us that Chapman's Bear was 'snowy', Mr
Kenner suggests that Eliot's is shuddering not with cold alone:
'there is a quaint tradition that the Bear's orgasm lasts nine
days'. I took the tip and, true enough, it all falls into place.

> These with a thousand small deliberations
> Protract the profit of their chilled delirium,
> Excite the membrane, when the sense has cooled . . .

(Or, 'A cold coming we had of it'.) Similarly,

> We have not reached conclusion, when I
> Stiffen in a rented house.

(Cf. what Crazy Jane said to the Bishop, last stanza.) It is all
extremely satisfying, though of course it makes 'Gerontion'
sound like a sort of super *Peyton Place*. 'After such knowledge'
(Eliot)—'a word with sexual and Biblical as well as epistemo-
logical contexts' (Kenner)—'what forgiveness?' (Eliot). After
such parlour games, what poetry?

But that is Mr Kenner at his least humorous and least humane.
His glossing of *The Waste Land* is considerably more tactful.
Whether 'The river's tent is broken' makes us think of 'broken
maidenheads' or of some deciduous ('shedding its wings after
copulation,' *C.O.D.*, my gloss) 'tunnel of love' is a matter of
personal sensibility. We may or may not feel that the word
'combinations' 'sounds a little finer than the thing it denotes'
or that 'carbuncular' touches the young man with glory. At
least we are interested to hear that Mr Kenner responds in these
ways. His handling of *Four Quartets* is even lighter-fingered,
while the 'Criticism' chapter is what book-reviewers call 'a
must', both for what he quotes and for what he says. 'Eliot

I

extended and generalised his *Egoist* manner into what was to be, until fame overtook him, his fundamental critical strategy: a close and knowing mimicry of the respectable.' Mr Kenner's references to Mr Eliot private and unpublished are authentically Possumistic in tone and flavour.

Speaking of mimicry—the newest mode of new criticism now that the heavy guns have all been fired and one has almost forgotten how the small still voices of the original creative writers sounded—Mr Kenner operates an urbane, mobile, Eliotic style, which is often amusing, sometimes illuminating, occasionally irritating. He is very funny in a fresh transatlantic way about Guy Fawkes Night, 'this patriotic emotion released by the circumstance that on a certain historical occasion nothing happened'. He is funny and enlightening on F. H. Bradley, funny on book reviewing, and not so funny on the *Encyclopaedia Britannica*, that 'compendium of organised illusion'. Dear me, how knowing we have grown! And that which we are knowing is Eliot. What Mr Kenner says is not always meaningful (for instance, his defence of the poetry of the plays, where he acts the clever lawyer hoodwinking a cowed jury), and some readers may feel about him and his subject that at times they have adapted themselves, as Eliot said of Swinburne's language, to 'an independent life of atmospheric nourishment'.

The Invisible Poet does not seek to explain—indeed, does not seem to recognise—the strange paradox of a poet who at times looks horror in the eye like a hero of myth and at other times shies away from human indelicacies like an old maid from a small boy watering a hedge. This is certainly not a pious book, but perhaps it is still insufficiently critical. There is something slightly emasculated about a procedure which, while glossing with enormous skill its subject's way of saying, makes next to no comment on what its subject says. Mr Kenner can be deliciously mordant, but generally about persons and institutions which Eliot swallowed up long ago. After all, and as Old Possum would be the first to admit, a cat may look at a king, even at what the blurb truthfully calls 'the regnant sensibility of our time'. Especially when, *pace* Mr Kenner's title, the king is eminently visible. (1960)

Telling Nothing

Eliot, it is believed, did not wish to be the subject of a biography. That was a vain wish, surely. It may serve to delay the inevitable, but if delay is to admit a succession of 'memoirs', it is advisable for a writer not merely not to discourage biographies but to insist that one should be produced as expeditiously as possible—and by a fellow-writer.

'It is becoming a critical truism to state that, without a knowledge of Eliot's tragic first marriage, a complete appreciation of the poems is totally impossible.' Perhaps a residual uneasiness has betrayed Mr Adamson into over-confidence. I doubt whether this is becoming a truism; I doubt even more whether it is true. We could have reconstructed Eliot's first marriage from his earlier poetry, had we wished. But why should we wish? If the animus against sex, the shrinking from the flesh, is felt to be artistically unaccounted for in his work, then no amount of 'explanation' imported from his life will rectify it artistically. In fact, early and late, Eliot's poetry is the expression of a strong personality (what he had to say about 'impersonality' is an essential ingredient of that personality), a distinctive and powerful way-of-seeing-things. Its difficulties are local: though subject to a diversity of interpretations deriving from a diversity of interpreters, he is not fundamentally an esoteric writer; his concerns were of the major kind.

The late Robert Sencourt and his editor are decent, respectful and nice-minded men, remote from the ignoble and ludicrous ambition to Tell All. Yet much of *T. S. Eliot: A Memoir* would surely have offended Eliot's sense of privacy, while he could hardly have been gratified by the surprisingly inept comments on his writing and that of others (Sencourt admired Alfred Noyes as a poetic innovator) or by the prose, stuffy or sanctimonious or vulgarly rapturous, which he has inspired in his old friend. There are some very odd sentences. 'Scrupulous as he was, Tom would never deny the existence of sex instinct either in himself or anybody else.' It would have been foolish to try. 'It is normal for a woman to enjoy her power to play upon the strings and nerves of manhood till they hasten the throbbing pulse with sensations of peculiar pleasure.' To offset his unchivalrous but unavoidable references to Vivien Eliot's abnormality, Sencourt stresses her normality in a mode reminiscent of *Peg's Paper*. 'Into this cheap room arrived a pimpled vulgar clerk, perhaps of a type Tom met at the bank ... What could be more sordid than an affair of this kind or the abortion engineered by Lou in the section preceding it?' There are worse things than sordidness: cold rightmindedness for instance. The 'engineer', incidentally, was Lil—not the nasty-tongued Lou, who presumably speaks for the rightminded here.

However, there is one excellent story. The French housekeeper who looked after John Hayward and Eliot in the 1950's was much impressed by the latter's sanctity. 'Mr Eliot était un homme très religieux,' she told Sencourt, 'il ne lisait jamais les journaux le dimanche.' (1971)

BETWEEN HÖLDERLIN
AND HIMMLER

IT is scarcely the case that we live in a time when literary conventions are so narrow and stifling that 'poetry' must become, for the poet, a dirty word. Far from it. Poetically, anything goes, and the louder the faster, though perhaps not very far. So the more one considers the title of Hans Magnus Enzensberger's volume of selected poems—with English translations facing the German text, except on one occasion—the more sadly irrelevant or even senseless it comes to seem.[1] People who don't read poems don't read poems.

In the longest piece here, 'summer poem', the phrase '*das ist keine kunst*' keeps recurring—'that's not art'. In a note the author describes the phrase as 'the traditional objection of a bourgeois aesthetic against every innovation'. True, such was the situation, once upon a time. But far more often today we hear the complaint 'but that's *art*', the false artist's by now traditional objection to the suggestion that art should be something more than a howl, a slash of paint or a tangle of old iron. The genuine artist—and there is clear evidence here of Enzensberger's genuineness—oughtn't to be wasting his time and energy on this sort of shadow-boxing.

Enzensberger has set his face against Rilke, Bach, Hölderlin ('what can we do / with everyone / who says hölderlin and means himmler'), seemingly because their work failed to prevent the Nazi extermination camps, because indeed some camp commandants were actually connoisseurs of music and poetry. Are Rilke, Bach and Hölderlin to blame for this? Should they have written only for good men to read? Maybe in a few score years the work of Enzensberger will be judiciously appreciated by the monsters of some new regime,

---

[1] *Poems for People Who Don't Read Poems*, by Hans Magnus Enzensberger, translated from the German by Michael Hamburger, Jerome Rothenberg and the Author.

whose withers are left unwrung, or are probably unwringable anyway?

Perhaps Rilke, at least, was too much the self-regarding artist, spinning literature out of his own guts, with too little concern for the guts of others. '*Hiersein ist herrlich*' ('to be here is glorious'), says Enzensberger, glancing with rather heavy irony at one of Rilke's best known and most willed announcements. The allusion comes in Enzensberger's 'man spricht deutsch', which plays angrily with the phraseology and appurtenances of the Economic Miracle. (A word of praise is due to the translators: here and elsewhere, thrown into a verbal bloodbath, they contrive to make on their own swings what they lose on the original roundabouts, as with 'on the bonny bonny banks we play blind man's buff'.) True, one expects a miracle to take place in a cowshed, on a mountain, by a lake side, at a tomb—and not, in economic guise, in the vicinity of gas chambers, not upon the ashes of incinerated thousands. When it does, you can scream with rage and horror, but the Miracle still stands, your screams won't make it fall down like the walls of Jericho. You must also speak clearly, and say what you want instead of this Miracle. It is natural in Enzensberger that the experience of the 'new Germany' should hurt all the worse because of the old Germany:

> this is a country different from any other . . .

> germany, my country, unholy heart of the nations,
> pretty notorious, more so every day,
> among ordinary people elsewhere . . .

> there i shall stay for a time,
> till i move on to the other people
> and rest, in a country quite ordinary,
> elsewhere,
> not here.

Is there any land left that is '*ganz gewöhnlich*' by what would seem to be Enzensberger's conception of the ordinary? And if there is, what on earth would he find to do in it?

A good deal of what Enzensberger cries out against in Germany is in fact universal. And some of it is trivial. Since the artist *must* select, anyway, it is best that he *does* select. And selection appears to be this poet's weak point. Embroidered napkins, whipped cream, wage negotiators, plastic bags, chambers of commerce, murderers' dens, bonus vouchers, chamois beard hats, coca-cola and arsenals, Rilke and Dior, branflakes and bombs, they all feature as expletives in a lengthy curse, all of equal weight apparently, or in the end of equal weightlessness. To be angry about everything is to be angry about nothing. Enzensberger's rage declines into rant, his fierce indignation into smashing-up-the-furniture. One thinks of Brecht's poems, and of his gift for selecting the one detail, the one image, the one reference which will tell all, or as much as he set out to tell.

The last poem in this book is called 'Joy', and it begins,

> she does not want me to speak of her
> she won't be put down on paper
> she can't stand prophets . . .

It is a more hopeful poem than most of Enzensberger's, for it ends by speaking of Joy's *'siegreiche flucht'* ('her long flight to victory'), but it is a little too abstract, too willed, and deficient in the urgency and the implied compassionateness of similar poems by Brecht, such as

> In meinem Lied ein Reim
> Käme mir fast vor wie Übermut
>
> (In my poetry a rhyme
> Seemed to me almost like presumption)

or

> Der Lachende
> Hat die furchtbare Nachricht
> Nur noch nicht empfangen
>
> (The man who laughs
> Has not yet heard the dreadful news).

Yet for me Enzensberger is at his best when at his nearest to Brecht, and when he eschews length, as in 'bill of fare', 'poem about the future', the grimly comic 'midwives' and (a very fine poem) 'the end of the owls':

> i speak for none of your kind,
> i speak of the end of the owls.
> i speak for the flounder and whale
> in their unlighted house . . .
> i speak for those who can't speak,
> for the deaf and dumb witnesses,
> for otters and seals,
> for the ancient owls of the earth.

These are Enzensberger's most moving, most impressive poems —and I don't mean (if indeed it means anything at all) 'aesthetically'. These, by implication, contain the horror and disgust of the longer pieces, but go beyond horror and disgust, not by annulling them, by selling out to 'art', but by assuring us that the poet is not himself merely a destroyer with a grievance against bigger and better destroyers. Here he is not making war but speaking, soberly and lucidly, of the pity of war. In his longer poems, Enzensberger's weapon is the blunderbuss, where it should rather be the rapier. Or is that too much like 'art'? In an age of nuclear weapons the rapier cannot be said to be noticeably less effective than the blunderbuss or the bludgeon, and it is certainly more discriminating. And the poet, unlike the atom bomb, ought to discriminate still. (1968)

DID NOBODY TEACH YOU?

On Stevie Smith

THE vivacious narrator of *Novel on Yellow Paper*, who claims to have written a long poem entitled 'La Fille de Minos et de Pasiphaë', declares a constitutional preference for Racine over Shakespeare. A French preference, obviously, and the reasons she gives are French (the admirer of Shakespeare will present much the same account as grounds for his admiration): Shakespeare's verse is 'conventional' whereas the feeling is 'so warm and so human and so disturbing', and for Pompey Casmilus this is an antithesis which makes her feel 'distraught and ill at ease'. Then there are too many complications in Shakespeare's plots, too many inessentials, too many (if beautiful) distractions. 'The plot of a tragedy must be bone-straight and simple.' Pompey has strong opinions about a number of serious matters, and distinct feelings (she is not unfeeling at all!), but she does not like a riot of emotion: 'I do not like it at all'. Thus she is at home with *Phèdre* because 'Racine is very serene, very severe, very austere and simple . . . And this tragedy is also very bracing . . . very strong and very inevitable and impersonal.'

These adjectives, or some of them, could be applied to Stevie Smith's own poetry. Severe, austere, simple, bracing, impersonal. If 'this is truly Greek, and what the Greek is', then Stevie Smith is somewhat Greek. If to be classical is not to be (in a number of senses of that peculiar adjective) romantic, then she is in some senses classical. Like these adjectives, she is equivocal, not half as simple as she seems. For instance, there is a sparsity of great expectations in her outlook, or so it would appear. The Frog Prince is 'fairly happy in a frog's doom':

> I have been a frog now
> For a hundred years

And in all this time
I have not shed many tears . . .

Why change? To have the *heavenly* time which the story
promises once the princess has kissed him, he must free himself
from his contentment, for perhaps it is part of the spell 'to make
much of being a frog', and open himself to disenchantment:

> Come, then, royal girl and royal times,
> Come quickly,
> I can be happy until you come
> But I cannot be heavenly,
> Only disenchanted people
> Can be heavenly.

The poem is not simple and straightforward, after all, because
of that ambiguous word *heavenly*, which is both flapper-talk
and terribly eschatological (or something else very serious), and
here, it seems, modulates from one sense into the other, so that
finally it is the 'romance' of living under a spell, in a frog's
paradise as it were, that is to be exposed, not the romance
which the fairy story holds out as the palace-living princess-
loving future. Finally, to stand a chance of being 'heavenly',
you must be a man, undeluded.

If in the upshot this poem doesn't have much to say one way
or the other about great expectations, it is an apt illustration of
something else: that (as no doubt in Racine and in the Greeks)
'bone-straight and simple' doesn't necessarily mean shallow or
obvious, and while you can usually dart through Miss Smith's
poems with immediate enjoyment, some of them are deep and
(though they make no overt demand in this direction) deserve
and repay considerable thought. Among such substantial
pieces are 'I had a dream. . .', 'The Last Turn of the Screw',
'The Airy Christ', 'Come on, Come back' and 'The Crown of
Gold'.

If classicism is avoidance of the romantic, then one can
adduce her best-known because most obvious attributes: the
perverse off-rhyming (she goes out of her way to rhyme im-
purely, but at other times thumps down on the most obvious

if pure rhyme), the inevitably comic and deflatory effect of rhyming English words with French, and the bathos which W. McGonagall achieved effortlessly but she had to work for. Thus 'Saffron' concludes on an inept rhyme, which reins in the reader abruptly, *and* with an austerely negative way-of-putting-it:

> Bice, Pale and Saffron but I love best
> Beautiful summer Saffron, running fast.
> Because this beautiful spirit should not be frozen
> And is furthest from it when she is saffron.

Lest 'Hymn to the Seal', in its celebration of 'God's creatures in their prime', should wax too grandiose, the middle stanza runs thus:

> When thou wast young thy coat
> Was pale with spots upon it,
> But now in single black it lies
> And thou, Seal, liest on it.

'The Small Lady' with her large washing machine, victim of a malicious witch, is shown as remonstrating in this way:

> 'Aroint thee, false witch!' cried the lady with a brave face,
> 'Human inventions help properly, magic is a disgrace.'

A good sentiment, surely, but somewhat reductively expressed. The philosophical dialogue between Eve and the Virgin Mary is left to continue, but the report on the proceedings terminates on a strong note of definitive inconclusiveness:

> And they talked until nightfall,
> But the difference between them was radical.

And in what is surely a very serious poem, 'A Man I am', with the reminiscence of Blake often remarked on in her work and a rather more pronounced flavour of the seventeenth century (particularly Herbert and Vaughan), the resonant lines

> But presently the spring broke in
> Upon the pastures of my sin

are followed by the deliberately flat

> My poor heart bled like anything,

and in turn this is succeeded by

> And falling ill, I soon grew worse.
> Until at last I cried on Him,
> Before whom angel faces dim,
> To take the burden of my sin
> And break my head beneath his wing.

Stevie Smith's Christianity—she described herself as an agnostic Anglican, and she seems to me to have known a lot about Christianity, what it was, or what it could be—was no Phantom Spiritual State, no theological preserve or Sunday subject, but very much part and parcel of everyday life. Perhaps the sensed kinship with George Herbert resides here.

'Unromantic' too are her reservations on the subject of Love. Or Love as it is generally written about. 'Anger's Freeing Power' tells of a raven who fancies himself a captive in a cell which has only three walls. The loving narrator cannot persuade the bird that in fact he is free to fly away, but then two other ravens come along and jeer at him in a nicely vulgar manner:

> You wretched bird, conceited lump
> You well deserve to pine and thump.

This treatment works wonders: 'Oh do I then? he says,' and off he flies to heaven's skies. The narrator is left to muse ruefully:

> Yet when I woke my eyes were wet
> To think Love had not freed my pet
>
> Anger it was that won him hence
> As only Anger taught him sense

> Often my tears fall in a shower
> Because of Anger's freeing power.

Here she is close to Blake, that unromantic romantic and angel-seeing realist: 'Damn braces. Bless relaxes', and 'The tygers of wrath are wiser than the horses of instruction'. Her Christ, too, is more tiger than lamb—'He is Noble, he is not Mild.'

While part of her is in sympathy with dreamers, for to dream is human, part of her remains cool, sceptical and admonitory, and sometimes with an effect of what Derwent May has called 'comic, forthright, moral knockabout':

> I'm sorry to say my dear wife is a dreamer,
> And as she dreams she gets paler and leaner.
> 'Then be off to your Dream, with his fly-away hat,
> I'll stay with the girls who are happy and fat.'

'Accidie poisons the soul stream,' as Pompey reminds us. Life has to go on, despite dreams and dreamers, and if the dreamer can be shaken into sense, then he or she should be. We observe how the poet passes with relief from 'Dear Female Heart':

> Dear Female Heart, I am sorry for you,
> You must suffer, that is all that you can do.
> But if you like, in common with the rest of the human race,
> You may also look most absurd with a miserable face—

to 'Alfred the Great':

> Honour and magnify this man of men
> Who keeps a wife and seven children on £2 10
> Paid weekly in an envelope
> And yet he never has abandoned hope.

Miss Smith could be grim. The woman chatting harmlessly on the omnibus in 'Northumberland House', it transpires, is on her way to a lunatic asylum: the poet characteristically employs the old non-euphemism. And the gentleman uttering pious sentiments over a grave—

> Farewell for ever, well for ever fare,
> The soul whose body lies beneath this stone!—

is revealed as the murderer:

> My hand brought *Filmer Smith* to this strait bed—
> Well, fare his soul well, fear not I the dead.

She can be grim—but she won't stand for any nonsense about abandoning hope. That would be *ignoble*. In what looks like steps in a campaign against received 'enlightened' opinion, she shows something of the terrifying honesty which Eliot ascribed to Blake. On one plane she seeks to rescue and rehabilitate the word 'pretty'. On another plane, the poem which begins

> A mother slew her unborn babe
> In a day of recent date
> Because she did not wish him to be born in a world
> Of murder and war and hate
> 'Oh why should I bear a babe from my womb
> To be broke in pieces by a hydrogen bomb?'

takes an unexpected, heterodox turn: we are not invited to sympathise with the mother and her 'tragic dilemma', but rather the opposite:

> I say this woman deserves little pity
> That she was a fool and a murderess
> Is a child's destiny to be contained by a mind
> That signals only a lady in distress?
>
> And why should human infancy be so superior
> As to be too good to be born in this world?
> Did she think it was an angel or a baa-lamb
> That lay in her belly furled?

At the very end there is, perhaps, another turn:

> How foolish this poor mother to suppose
> Her act told us aught that was not murderous

(As, item, That the arrogance of a half-baked mind
Breeds murder; makes us all unkind.)

Makes us *all* unkind—including the poet herself.

No, Miss Smith was not notably trusting. She didn't altogether trust the Muse. The Muse deserts you because you
have complained that she doesn't speak loudly enough—and
you hear her howling and muttering behind the door. Then
you search for her by night and day, and you cry upon the
Lord to give her back to you:

> He did repent. I have her now again
> Howling much worse, and oh the door is open.

The poet may be happy, healthy, in himself, but his poetry
can be unhappy, distressing himself and others:

> My heart leaps up with streams of joy,
> My lips tell of drouth:
> Why should my heart be full of joy
> And not my mouth?
>
> I fear the Word, to speak or write it down,
> I fear all that is brought to birth and born:
> This fear has turned my joy into a frown.

Not very trusting, but she was never cynical. And not hard so
much as brisk, and especially brisk in situations which require
briskness and a touch of bracing tartness. For all the dippiness,
she was a moralist firm in degree and central in kind, and a
moralist in the best sense, for she felt while she judged. The
engaging combination of overt sternness with underlying gentle-
ness is shiningly present in 'Valuable' ('After reading two para-
graphs in a newspaper'), which I quote in full:

> All these illegitimate babies . . .
> Oh girls, girls,
> Silly little cheap things,
> Why do you not put some value on yourselves,

Learn to say, No?
Did nobody teach you?
Nobody teaches anybody to say No nowadays,
People should teach people to say No.

Oh poor panther,
Oh you poor black animal,
At large for a few moments in a school for young
   children in Paris,
Now in your cage again,
How your great eyes bulge with bewilderment,
There is something there that accuses us,
In your angry and innocent eyes,
Something that says:
I am too valuable to be kept in a cage.

Oh these illegitimate babies!
Oh girls, girls,
Silly little valuable things,
You should have said, No, I am valuable,
And again, It is because I am valuable
I say, No.

Nobody teaches anybody they are valuable nowadays.

Girls, you are valuable,
And you, Panther, you are valuable,
But the girls say: I shall be alone
If I say 'I am valuable' and other people do not say
   it of me,
I shall be alone, there is no comfort there.
No, it is not comforting but it is valuable,
And if everybody says it in the end
It will be comforting. And for the panther too,
If everybody says he is valuable
It will be comforting for him.

Miss Smith wanted happiness to exist where it possibly
could. Indeed, she would have liked to see Phèdre happily
married to Hippolytus: 'I think it might have been a go. . . .'
But life, she knows, is a struggle, no matter what you might
think you would like it to be instead:

Ceux qui luttent ce sont ceux qui vivent.
And down here they luttent a very great deal indeed.
But if life be the desideratum, why grieve, ils vivent.

And though she has asked—more precisely, 'a little wind
sneaking along That was older than all and infamously strong'
has asked—'Will Man ever face fact and not feel flat?', in
practice man is often seen to rise superior to his myths. Even
to the cruel story of Eve:

> . . . there is this to be said still:
> Life would be over long ago
> If men and women had not loved each other
> Naturally, naturally,
> Forgetting their mythology
> They would have died of it else
> Long ago, long ago,
> And all would be emptiness now
> And silence.

Man sometimes does contrive to face fact and not fall flat on
his face, even to live not without honour, so that on balance

> It is his virtue needs explaining,
> Not his failing.
>
> Away, melancholy,
> Away with it, let it go.

As for eccentricity and quaintness, Miss Smith's themes are
commonly the large ones, central to the human condition.
Extremely interesting, and sufficient to dispose of any suggestion of her being a 'naïf', are her reflections on death and suicide.
The possibility, or the availability, of suicide is a great strength-
ener, Pompey muses; every child should be told, 'Things may
easily become more than I choose to bear'—

that 'choose' is a grand old burn-your-boats phrase that will put
beef into the little one, and you see if it doesn't bring him to a
ripe old age. If he doesn't in the end go off natural I shall be

K

surprised . . . See what it's done for me. I'm twice the girl I was
that lay crying and waiting for death to come at that convalescent
home. No, when I sat up and said: Death has got to come if I call
him, I never called him, and never have.

And so, in the terms of one simple little verse, you look at the
bottle of aspirin when you feel mournful, you reflect that two
hundred will free you from anxiety—but you don't do more
than look. Death you should think of as a friend: though you
can call upon a friend, you should not impose upon him—and
moreover Death is also a 'great prince'. Miss Smith valued
propriety and decorum. The argument is by no means un-
subtle. On the one side,

> a time may come when a poet or any person
> Having a long life behind him, pleasure and sorrow,
> But feeble now and expensive to his country
> And on the point of no longer being able to make a
>   decision
> May fancy Life comes to him with love and says:
> We are friends enough now for me to give you death;
> Then he may commit suicide, then
> He may go.

On the other side (as in 'Mr Over'), it may be a devil's voice
that cries, 'Happy Happy the dead,' for God says this:

> In man is my life, and in man is my death,
> He is my hazard, my pride and my breath,
> I sought him, I wrought him, I pant on his worth,
> In him I experience indeterminate growth.

> Oh Man, Man, of all my animals dearest,
> Do not come till I call, though thou weariest first.

Neville Braybrooke recalls Stevie Smith having said to him
towards the end of her life: 'People think because I never
married, I know nothing about the emotions. When I am dead
you must put them right. I loved my aunt.' One could not for
long suspect her of such ignorance. She was no *cenobite*—to use

one of Pompey's favourite names for unfavourite things: 'two
diseases we have right here that the modern world is suffering
from—*dictators* like I said and *cenobites* like I said too . . .'. In a
short poem called 'Man is a Spirit' she points out snappishly
that, even so, the spirit-guest oughtn't to wrinkle up his nose
at the flesh-host who serves him well when the wind blows.
And obviously she agrees with Ormerod when he maintains
that he can have knowledge of God both before life and after
death, but that here in temporal life, and only in temporal life,
is permitted 'A place where man might impinge upon man,
And be subject to a thousand and one idiotic distractions'—

> I knew, and shall know again, the name of God, closer
>   than close;
> But now I know a stranger thing,
> That never can I study too closely, for never will it
>   come again—
> Distractions and the human crowd.

There is a time and a place for everything. Ripeness is all,
ripeness of time and rightness of place.

In its essence Stevie Smith's poetry is uncluttered, and hence
must leave out, for instance, the reservations and modifications
and clarifications which a denser and slower-moving writing
admits. But it leaves out what it could not accommodate and
still be the kind of poetry it is: and that is all it leaves out. A
reader may well prefer other kinds of poetry, of course, but he
cannot make out that her poetry is one of those other kinds
which has somehow 'gone wrong'. When it succeeds, it obeys
its own laws, and they are not unduly restrictive. At moments
she is like a lot of other poets—I would add Hardy, de la Mare,
Ogden Nash, Edward Lear, the creators of ballads, of hymns,
of nursery rhymes, to those already noted—but finally, in the
totality of her work, she is simply like herself. At the worst
her poems are rather dull, and one asks 'So what?': that is the
way of failing of her kind of poetry. I think she fails surprisingly rarely, especially if we read the poems in bulk, when
among themselves they provide their own qualifications and
refine their arguments. To say this is to remind oneself that a

part of her best work, at all events her most *own*, hasn't been touched on here. And simply because there seems to be nothing to say about it: children are likely to enjoy it unworryingly, it engages adults and yet leaves them baffled and a little uneasy. It is not amenable to interpretation or conducive to moralising. And one thinks of Pompey's sharp remarks on clever talk about books and pictures and how 'you want to keep very mum-o, and you want to keep the smarties off, oh yes they can read now, and very cunning they are the way they pick things up, very quick and cunning, much fiercer about it they are . . .'. Perhaps it is appropriate to end with one such poem, 'Voices about the Princess Anemone':

> Underneath the tangled tree
> Lies the pale Anemone.
>
> She was the first who ever wrote
> The word of fear, and tied it round her throat.
>
> She ran into the forest wild
> And there she lay and never smiled.
>
> Sighing, Oh my word of fear
> You shall be my only dear.
>
> They said she was a princess lost
> To an inheritance beyond all cost.
>
> She feared too much they said, but she says, No,
> My wealth is a golden reflection in the stream below.
>
> She bends her head, her hands dip in the water
> Fear is a band of gold on the King's daughter.

(1971)

CHILDREN'S HOUR

The Stepney Poets

THE brave infant of Saguntum celebrated in Jonson's ode, being half out of his mother's womb, looked at what was around him and hastily went back:

> As, could they but life's miseries foresee,
> No doubt all infants would return like thee.

The children in *Stepney Words*[1] seem to have acquired a sense of life's miseries rather early too, but they are more resigned, the poetic licence of the infant of Saguntum is not for the likes of them. One of them wonders whether the world outside is bright or dull:

> I will not be able to get back into the womb if
>   it is dull.
> It is just a chance i will have to take,

while another tells himself,

> The security of the womb is no longer mine,
> I must look for something else to see me through
>   my first strange, lonely years.

After birth comes loneliness, boredom and perhaps un-wantedness:

> It's the same every night.
> Me dad's on the booze
> Me mum's watching tele . . .

[1] A Collection of Poetry by Stepney Children aged 11 to 15 years, compiled by Christopher Searle.

But there are cheerful interludes, the simple enjoyment of swinging to and fro, of getting sunburnt in the holidays, of watching kittens and pigeons, and the less straightforward pleasure of watching other animals (who sometimes remind you of man). There is a skilful contemporary ballad which begins,

> Ten little football fans
> Making rude signs,
> One swore at a policeman
> Then there were nine,

and keeps it up right to the end:

> One little football fan
> Glad his team had won,
> Argued with some other fans
> Then there were none.

There is a quite complexly touching poem about a boy saved from drowning by someone whose kitten he was trying to rescue, and an oddly striking poem about a lonely dustman whose 'only truthful friends are the rubbish':

> Everyday my friends are thrown into the streets
>   and put into iron cages,
> And they rely on me to take them out of a dreadful,
>   dirty and awkward world of horror.
> Then along comes a different world.
> It's a dust-cart.
> Then once more my friends rush against me
>   and I throw them into a world of darkness.
> But now we are on strike, I see my friends
>   wherever I go.

Most of the children don't think much of Stepney, but one girl likes the place without being able to give reasons: 'Everything in Stepney has its disadvantages / But I like it.' And—for more wisdom than is comfortable to observe comes out of the mouth of these babes—living in Stepney at least makes one's memories of Wapping shine brightly. It's not so very unnatural that no one should like school, but one child does describe a good school, whether real or imaginary, where there are

> No rules,
> Just a pleasant, quiet atmosphere between parents,
>   teachers, and us, the children.

The other common topics are sombre, and they don't have to be searched out:

> we knock down houses
> and we build car parks
> Why don't we build houses?

And more longingly:

> I live in old flats. . .
> I wish I could make into a brand new home
> with a drive way that never ends
> and doors were as big as the house itself
> with a door knocker that no one would touch because
> they thought it was too valuable, the house would
> have two swimming pools of course olympic size.

Pakistanis lament their lot, abroad and at home, and a white child utters the final word on the subject of colour:

> It's not his fault
>   he's black.
> Nor is it our fault
>   we're white.

There is only one poem about war ('Men's bodies lie rotting in the hot Egyptian sun, / And at home all mothers are wondering if it is their son'), which is not surprising in children of this age, especially since they live on a battlefield of their own. Then the wheel comes full circle, and they write about old age, when the loneliness of childhood, the isolation and lack of understanding, return. It is as if the children find in talking about old people a less embarrassing way of talking about themselves: 'I am old and frightened / in this darkened world . . .'. But at least the old have their memories, ambiguous as these may be, and some of them win a sort of respect for their obstinate independence, the freedom of their eccentricity—there's no slick talk about 'doing one's own thing' in this book!—and one child holds out for them a vague hope of a kind rare here:

> He is old and his time probably up
> It can't be put back,
> Maybe in some other time and place
> Time won't matter anymore.

Is the selection of poems unbalanced? For our peace of mind we must hope so, or else tell ourselves that a sad tale's always been best for poetry. But what is inescapably painful, and frightening, about these laconic verses, and finally most impressive, is the children's clear-sightedness, their unwavering gaze—or, at any rate, the total absence of illusions. Not for them, or not for long, the escape into fantasy:

> Fantasy is so unreal
> But it's nice to dream.
> Fact puts the truth to you
> so it's quite cruel.

> People escape to fields of fantasy
> because they can't face the truth,
> but, never mind, the time will come
> for them to see the facts . . .

And their attitude to drugs is regretful and admonitory, not at all permissive. Their lack of enthusiasm has a simple, pragmatic and valid reason—drugs don't work. 'Gale is dead':

> In prison now she hears girls talk
> About drugs

And the way life would look
She thought it sounded better . . .

While another girl writes, of the needle, the jab in the arm,

Reality is going, the fantasy world
Is appearing in their eyes
The dream of how they want the world to be
Will come to them soon.

But their world is seen in a haze of dreams,
It would never, never be true
But when you've tried to escape once,
You will have to escape over
                                   over
                                        over
                                             again.

Stoicism is difficult to take in children, for we like to think of
it as a hard-earned adult virtue, even when we remember how
we needed to call on it, or were driven into it, in our own
childhood. Yet it may be that, after the experiences of school,
nothing in later life can seem so very bad—unless you are a
blackie, an unmarried mother, a blind man, a soldier, or a
lonely old person.

These are bleak little verses, utterly uncaring of the attractions of form or stylistic invention and equally devoid of
fashionable gimmickry, plainly explicit and yet never noisy.
Still wondering whether the collection was unbalanced, the
choice tendentious, I compared them with finalists of the same
age-group in the 1970 *Daily Mirror* Children's Literary Com-
petition. These latter poems were markedly more sophisticated
in thought, feeling and technique, more 'modernistic', more
romantic, more fanciful, more humorous, more self-interested;
they ranged more widely in subject-matter, there were more
'nature poems' among them, and also more references to
formal war. Yet they too evidenced the same concerns, if not
in such concentration, the same personal and social discontents,
secular rather than divine. And they often hit harder than the
Stepney children, as if their authors had more hope of setting

things to rights, as if their expectations were a size or two
larger, perhaps. This, from a 15-year-old girl:

> Why are you crying, child?
> No one will listen.
> On your starved, hungry cheeks
> Two teardrops glisten.
> We do not care for you—
> Run child away!
> Why should we think of you?
> Don't spoil today.
>
> Think of the cheques we sent
> (Second-class post)
> That will mean food for them
> Needing it most.
> You only live nearby:
> You can't be poor . . .
> There's always the dole for you
> If nothing more.
>
> Come to the Church, my child.
> We'll give you prayers—
> Then when you die you can
> Know that God cares.
> We won't perform his job—
> He does it best.
> There's others in need, my child.
> Think of the rest ! . . .

Another girl, 16 years old, chose a 'Stepney' theme but lashed
out far more savagely:

> Long time ago, too long ago for us to care,
> A foolish man said, 'Love your neighbour,'
> How little that man knew.
> My neighbour has no frigidaire, no TV, no new car.
> My neighbour's clothes are cast-offs or pinched from God
>   knows where . . .
> My neighbour lives in a crowded slum

Shared with rats and lice.
My neighbour can't speak English and her children will
    not learn.
They're not worth help. Who'd want to know?
My neighbour is a world apart. My neighbour's black.

Besides their smarter finish, the *Daily Mirror* entries are
obviously more varied in subject and style. But then, they
don't all come from one school, they don't all come from
Stepney. Whatever the criteria by which the book was compiled, *Stepney Words* is evenly balanced as far as its somewhat
Spartan literary quality goes, and consistent in its standard of
clarity and directness. Perhaps the school governors ought to
have found consolation in those facts. Otherwise, to make use
of Wilfred Owen's words, these poems are to this generation
in no sense consolatory. (1971)

O ALTITUDO!

Poet, Poem and Reader

STANLEY BURNSHAW'S long and closely-knit book,
The Seamless Web, opens with the declaration that 'poetry
begins with the body and ends with the body'. Like the snake
with its tail in its mouth, it closes with the same sentence,
adding 'It begins in one and ends in another.' In between a lot
happens or nothing happens: rather, a large number of fascinating questions connected with the poet-poem and poem-
reader relationships are raised, discussed intelligently and coolly,
and gently dropped back into that dark and unchartable sea
from which they came. Or, another way of putting it, in
between there is a well-chosen anthology of what poets, critics,
philosophers and psychologists have had to say about the
nature of art, how it comes about and what it does. Some of
Mr Burnshaw's own contributions are worthy of the company
they keep.

But as an argument? If this book is an argument, it comes
to no conclusion, or to so many conclusions as to amount to
the same thing. To have come to clear and single conclusions,
Mr Burnshaw would have had to limit himself severely or else
to cheat, or of course to be simple. The variety of factors involved in the genesis of a literary work may not be infinite,
but it is not far off. The variety of effects produced by a variety
of poems on a variety of readers may not be infinite, but it is
quite near. Compared with the exploration of art, the exploration of the moon is a weekend assignment for schoolboys.

The intellectually myopic are not so likely, I suppose, to be
blinded with science. Which may be why I found Mr Burnshaw's physiological, biological, cerebral and zoological ex-
cursuses less illuminating than they were meant to be. The use
in artistic investigation of scientific procedure and parallels is
nearly always a mistake, if a well-intentioned one: the outcome
is a rather sorry thing by the standards of scientific discourse,

so that all the champion of the arts can say, lamely, is that everything has been explained except what matters. It has to be added that Mr Burnshaw's concern is not with poetry as ersatz fodder for scientific methodology, but with poetry as an activity of the most complex and indeed most momentous kind, and his dealings with it are a good deal more delicate than those of Richards's *Principles of Literary Criticism*.

A poem comes out of the poet's total organism, psycho-physical, mind-body, and goes into the reader's total organism . . . . Mr Burnshaw's first chapter is rich in expert witness, yet for all its recondite detail, it tells us little we didn't know before. It doesn't tell us as much (or as vividly) as Lawrence does in his lively, casual-seeming piece, 'Why the Novel Matters':

> Now I absolutely flatly deny that I am a soul, or a body, or a mind, or an intelligence, or a brain, or a nervous system, or a bunch of glands, or any of the rest of these bits of me. The whole is greater than the part. And therefore, I, who am man alive, am greater than my soul, or spirit, or body, or mind, or consciousness, or anything else that is merely a part of me. I am a man, and alive, I am man alive . . .

Among so much diversity of experience, some phenomena are recurrent: for example, the insistence by poets that they are being 'used', whether the force that uses them is called Inspiration or Unconsciousness, the White Goddess or the Dark Gods. You cannot write poetry just by wanting to, it comes or it doesn't: and 'coming' suggests a source outside the will, a 'giver'. But what about revision or re-vision, that which occurs in the course of what Mr Burnshaw calls 'reconstituted vision'? For unhappily not everything is always (or even often) given . . . . Does the poet agree with Frost that 'if the sound is right the sense will take care of itself'? This proposition could as well be reversed, though perhaps no better reversed, since 'sound' and 'sense' are not simple and separate categories. Does the poet, along with Mallarmé, 'yield the initiative to the words' and keep the obtrusive will in abeyance? Mr Burnshaw points out very justly that 'any such model of compliance omits the all-too-human in a writer'. The most 'inspired', the most unselfconscious writing is frequently the most embarrassingly self-ish. The will, sometimes after all a force for decency, collaborating with the analytical intellect, needs to obtrude: something must seek to moderate the whinings of the Unconscious, must open the poem to other people. Not infrequently the 'given' is a present from loving Us to Our beloved Selves. The conclusion Mr Burnshaw reaches is that between the simple extremes of Involuntary and Voluntary there is an infinite number of gradations, of permutations and combinations. As so often in this book, we are left with a paradox whose contradictions all speak truth: the poet who said, 'If poetry comes not as naturally as the leaves to a tree, it had better not come at all' is one whose worksheets are 'a monument of "conscious artistry".'

It was Keats who defined 'Negative Capability' as 'when a man is capable of being in uncertainties, mysteries, doubts, without any irritable reaching after fact and reason'. Though almost superhumanly free from irritability, Mr Burnshaw is certainly reaching after fact and hoping to catch a few reasons. But he takes his failures with a good grace—he is a practitioner of poetry himself—as if he knows that most of what is catchable in this queer sea has been caught already and thrown back in to grow and prosper in its proper element. A sentence characteristic of him is this: 'The foregoing sentences . . . are cumbersome, finical; but to write down even the comprehensive little that may surely be said of a poem and to convey its indispensable at-onceness would require a book-long sentence.'

In other connections (all of them connected, for Mr Burnshaw's subject is an organic whole) the situation is much the same: opposites are both right; without contraries there would be no progression; not *either or* but a larger or smaller proportion of both or all three or four or five or. . . . Thus, the coexistence of cultural diversity (and linguistic differences) with human sameness (and similarities in 'language behaviour') . . . . Thus, the apparent paradox inherent in 'the pleasantness of the unpleasant in art'—of which Mr Burnshaw makes rather heavy weather, as if, for once, he does suspect 'pain' and 'pleasure' of being true and unrelated opposites . . . . And then there is the problem of belief, whether the reader can and does suspend his disbelief and in his reading 'go along with' views and doctrines from which he would ordinarily dissent. At times 'belief' matters a lot, at others it doesn't matter at all. Mr Burnshaw cites an excellent instance: 'A non-believer accepts the poem-prayer to the Sungod of Egypt but recoils from a Soviet Asia folkpoem which has changed the name of a traditional deity to "Lenin".' I think we have to agree with him that if we read the *Divine Comedy* 'purely as fictive art or unsignificant fantasy,' then we are not reading the *Divine Comedy*. . . . Belief/disbelief is a part of our total organism which it would scarcely seem possible to deposit in a pigeon-hole before we pass through the library turnstile! But the more one thinks about it, the more exhaustingly complicated the problem seems. Why is it, for instance, that the present writer, a non-believer, can enter into the body of George Herbert's poetry with what seems to him like reasonable ease and yet feels excluded from much of the *Four Quartets*? No doubt there are many answers in many specific cases, but there is no answer which is simultaneously utterable and applicable to sufficient poems and sufficient readers to amount to a 'contribution to knowledge'.

> A poem should not mean
> But be,

said Archibald MacLeish, and Mr Burnshaw adds, truly I believe, that if there isn't something in the poem that makes 'some acceptable type of sense' at once, then the reader will turn away without further ado. And so MacLeish can be inverted: 'A poem before it can "be" for a reader must "mean".' Mallarmé's epigram that poems are made not with ideas but with words is equally reversible. The original saying was useful in its time, the inversion is more salutary today. Another witticism we would like to re-structure is Gide's 'good sentiments make bad literature'. These generalisations by poets and critics are half-truths or, rather, wholly true in certain circumstances, wholly untrue in others. *Aperçus* are like proverbs, they rely on the context for their truth and relevance. Sometimes 'look before you leap' is a timely warning; at other times 'he who hesitates is lost' is valuable advice. The only absolute answer to Mr Burnshaw's dilemmas is: 'it all depends'.

Here and there one feels like adding one's own reservations to Mr Burnshaw's. Elsewhere one finds oneself confirming him with anecdotes from one's own experience. On the subject of 'word music', Mr Burnshaw points out that 'consonants and vowels do not exist as independent entities', and the word is 'sense-and-sonality'. This made me think of the eager student who claims in one essay that a succession of 's's' creates 'an atmosphere of soft, silken luxury', and in the next that a succession of 's's' creates 'an atmosphere of sinisterness and serpentine malice'. Without sense, sonality is nothing—or, if we are to live up to Mr Burnshaw's standard of circumspection, next to nothing.

In discussing the occasional need for extraneous knowledge, especially biographical, in understanding a poem, Mr Burnshaw remarks that without knowing that its author spoke as an active Communist at a particular time, the reader of Brecht's 'An die Nachgeborenen' 'could make only vague emotional sense of its confiding plea to posterity'. When an English translation of this poem was set recently as a practical criticism exercise for Singapore University students, one of them opined that it came from a released political detainee (perhaps the prearranged text of the TV recantation), and another that it was written by one of those Students' Unionists who are always finding fault with everything (a conservative citizen's conception, maybe, of a potential detainee). A poet sometimes assumes that the personal circumstances in which a poem originated will somehow survive alongside the poem—but then, if they did, there would be little need for the editorial footnote or the teacher of literature. When one is already engaged by 'some acceptable type of sense'—as I think is the case with this poem of Brecht's—one is ready to investigate background or biography, one actively wants to. Our quarrel is with the poem which expects the reader to do the donkeywork in the absence of the dangling carrot.

Mr Burnshaw invites expert attention, and perhaps readers

more expert, more knowledgeable, might detect faults in the careful unfolding of his argument. One passage made me stop and doubt. He states that 'not a single metaphor can be found in a great many excellent Chinese poems,' and he cites Waley's translation of a piece by Emperor Wu-ti.[1] Chinese scholars deny that metaphor is less prominent in Chinese poetry than in Western verse, and some doubt whether Wu-ti is a sufficiently excellent poet for his practice to be adduced as an 'excellent' example of anything Chinese. Mr Burnshaw is talking about a particular translation, a modern one, and not about Wu-ti's poem, and I suspect that if he had happened upon a Victorian translation, he would have found himself making a very different generalisation about Chinese poetry! This lapse is the stranger in view of Mr Burnshaw's firm objection in a later chapter to 'imitations' ('neither translations nor original poems but a species of improvisation') and his caveat on the subject of translation: 'I believe every verse translation should be accompanied . . . with a literal one in prose or a trot, for the protection of the reader and the author.'

Mr Burnshaw is describing rather than prescribing, and descriptions, he points out, are not explanations. Such, as we have noted, is the nature of the subject. But this consideration doesn't save the protracted urbanity of attitude, the scrupulously maintained judiciousness, from proving slightly tedious in the long run. Half-way through the long run I came across a passage in Ruth Pitter's preface to her recent *Poems 1926-1966* which impressed me with its actuality, its sense of a human voice, a sense which Mr Burnshaw's more scientific prose is rather deficient in:

I think a real poem, however simple its immediate content, begins and ends in mystery. It begins in that secret movement of the poet's being in response to the secret dynamism of life. It continues as a structure made of and evolved from and clothed in the legal tender and common currency of language; perhaps the simpler the better, so that the crowning wonder, if it comes, may emerge clear of hocus-pocus. (I think it is important to make the plain

[1] A solecism, since *ti* signifies 'Emperor'; therefore either 'Wu-ti' or 'Emperor Wu'.

L

meaning of the words as clear as possible, but it cannot always be made entirely clear. Our only obscurities, I feel, should be those we are driven into; then a sort of blessing may descend, making such obscurity magical.)

Granted that obscurity and indefiniteness of meaning pose yet another complex problem, one might still like someone to get up and ask that poems should customarily stand on their own feet—I am not now thinking of the biographical difficulty in Brecht's poem, for instance—to ask that the poet should do the work, his fair share of it, and not leave it to the researching reader to seek clues on other ground. As Miss Pitter suggests, our only obscurities should be those we are driven into. It is all very well for the Japanese to practise 'indefiniteness' in their conventional forms, since the reader knows what the indefiniteness conventionally signifies. It is less well when contemporary practitioners in the West seek sanctimonious refuge in dot-dot-dot-from their own lack of significance. The poet should be a maker, not a source of fragments for someone else to stick together.

The Seamless Web probably does as much as it could possibly do, given its spinner's exquisite manners. What leaves me rather disconcerted is that the reading of it took me longer and required a considerably greater effort of will than the reading of any of Dickens's longer novels or a sizable portion of *Paradise Lost*. For this looks like another paradox . . . . Art is already long—should talk about art, however intelligent, be longer? At all events, Mr Burnshaw's readers will want to associate themselves with his estimate of the continuing *importance* of art for mankind. In his closing remarks on the conflict in the mind between 'diencephalon' and 'cerebral cortex', or between primal forces and civilised forces, he proposes that one truce between them is *art*, when 'certain innermost needs of the organism fulfil themselves through imaginative creations'. The mystery—of the needs and how they are fulfilled—remains. Perhaps it is meant to. (1970)

NO CHEER FOR DEMOCRACY

'WHY is it that great creative artists can totally reject a liberal, democratic, humanitarian society, and prefer a cruel, authoritarian, bellicose society?'[1] The literary critics, as Mr Harrison (who doesn't appear to be one himself) points out, have largely evaded the question, by talking about style and technique rather than ideas, or by assuming that what the writer says refers to and exists in some other (and presumably better) world than ours and so has no connection with the concentration camps down the road. In short, by readily granting a comprehensive variety of poetic licence. 'Now, for the poet, he nothing affirmeth, and therefore he never lieth . . . The poet never maketh any circles about your imagination, to conjure you to believe for true what he writeth'—and certainly not for *politically* true. Understandably, that stout liberal humanist, William Empson, furnishes the book with an introduction, in which he remarks very pertinently that he has 'never found an opponent giving a telling example to prove that a man ought not to attempt the estimate which Bentham recommends'.

Mr Harrison's heart is in the right place, and he manages to be humane to the least humanitarian of his reactionaries, but unhappily his treatment of the subject is too superficial to be much more than another evasion of its real complexities. Granted that critics are wrong in slurring over subject-matter and ideas as if literature (and poetry especially) didn't need to be 'about' anything and was likely to be pretty vulgar if it was. Even so, Mr Harrison doesn't acknowledge the true mystery which surrounds this matter of a poet's or a novelist's *ideas* as embodied in a poem or a novel and the dubiousness of extracting them and setting them out as plain straightforward statement, political, religious or ethical. There is something in what Sidney said: the poet doesn't affirm, he tells you at the

[1] *The Reactionaries*, by John R. Harrison.

outset that he is writing poetry, not addressing a massed rally at Nuremberg. There *is* style, after all, there is tone, there are conventions. To search through Yeats for fascist tendencies is as rewarding as combing *Tristram Shandy* or *Ulysses* for smut. No doubt something can be retrieved, but it will be sadly dissimilar from hard-core pornography or the extermination of the Jews.

One personal instance. I have an immense admiration for Herbert's poems, a measured liking for Hopkins's, a non-appreciation of considerable stretches of *Four Quartets* and a pronounced dislike for Francis Thompson. And yet, at least for a non-Christian, these writers would seem to have a fair amount in common as regards their beliefs, their ideas. As the Japanese say, the water that a cow drinks turns to milk, the water that a snake drinks turns to venom. Returning to Sidney's defence of truthless poets: Yeats's dying aristocracy never lived, it is like Rilke's unicorn, 'the animal which is not'—

> Not there, because they loved it, it behaved
> as though it were . . .

Lawrence's 'Mexico' is a comparable phenomenon, and Mr Harrison tells us that 'for one whose "Englishness is his very vision" to pick Mexico, of all places, as the end of the trail leading to the regeneration of European society, is almost beyond serious consideration'. Politicians cannot abide a metaphor: they are concerned with facts. We recall Cleopatra's magnificent speech after the death of Antony.

> His legs bestrid the ocean, his rear'd arm
> Crested the world: his voice was propertied
> As all the tuned spheres . . .

Turning to Dolabella, she asks,

> Think you there was, or might be such a man
> As this I dreamt of?

Mr Harrison, like Dolabella, like any politician, would answer, 'Gentle madam, no'. Here he is not allowing art the evocation of the impossible. Elsewhere he expects impossibilities of it, when he complains that 'Lawrence cannot convincingly describe an ideal relationship'.

It is in developing his case against Yeats that Mr Harrison seems least convincing. 'He wanted a period of authoritarian rule to destroy the influence of a century or more of liberalism and democracy, and he saw in fascism the nearest approach to what he wanted.' Yeats's poetry can only be assimilated to fascism as we have known it (and as Yeats in the 1920's and early 1930's hadn't) by ignoring the humour and the irony in it—qualities which make writers unreliable as allies of no matter what political party. 'Yeats is prepared to let the majority remain illiterate as long as a few good poets are produced,' says Mr Harrison, adducing these lines from 'Among School Children':

> The children learn to cipher and to sing,
> To study reading-books and histories,
> To cut and sew, be neat in everything
> In the best modern way.

For a 60-year-old public man, this doesn't seem too discreditably reactionary; he even manages to smile, too. Rueful, resigned, gentle, even tender—in tone the stanza is far removed from John Betjeman's carping verse, which is simple-minded enough to be described as political statement:

> . . . many a cultivated hour they pass
> In a fine school with walls of vita-glass.
> Civics, eurhythmics, economics, Marx,
> How-to-respect-wild-life-in-National-Parks;
> Plastics, gymnastics—thus they learn to scorn
> The old thatch'd cottages where they were born.

It is precisely through not toeing a party-line, any party-line, that imaginative writers can illuminate those patches of experience or of possibility which political ideologies prefer to

leave unexamined for the immediate good of the cause. 'Ireland
shall get her freedom and you still break stone': that comment
might seem insulting to the national aspirations of a subject
people. Actually it has a prophetic truth about it, as the people
of newly independent countries are discovering—not to
mention, of course, its metaphorical truth, its universal and
timeless personal application. Mr Harrison is not too strong
on the facts of reading. In his recent book, *Beyond Culture*,
though preoccupied with similar doubts about the whole
tendency of modern literature, Lionel Trilling wrote conced-
ingly,

> I have yet to meet the student committed to an altruistic politics
> who is alienated from Stephen Dedalus by that young man's
> disgust with political idealism, just as I have yet to meet the
> student from the most disadvantaged background who feels
> debarred from what Yeats can give him by the poet's slurs upon
> shopkeepers or by anything else in his inexhaustible fund of
> snobbery.

Wyndham Lewis, the next on the list, is a very different
kettle of fish, and a fishier one. He *was* a political writer: I don't
think he was a *great* writer. From Lawrence, and particularly
from *The Plumed Serpent*, Mr Harrison quotes some horrific
passages, which one must simply say one disagrees with or
finds utterly repugnant. They cannot be dismissed as artistic
parable, because they are quite explicit. Cipriano's words to
Kate could be taken as metaphorical, as a human insight: 'The
bit of horror is like the sesame seed in the nougat, it gives the
sharp wild flavour. It is good to have it there.' But, as Mr
Harrison points out, the poetry materialises into murder, condoned by Kate on the grounds that it makes Cipriano a good
lover.

> When she thought of him and his soldiers, tales of swift cruelty
> she had heard of him: when she remembered his stabbing the
> three helpless peons, she thought: Why should I judge him?
> He is of the gods . . . What do I care if he kills people? His flame
> is young and clean.

Even so, even as one shares Mr Harrison's alarm, the suspicion grows that a decent, democratic, humanist line, imposed on literature at all effectively, would constitute a formidable tyranny! The dark side of the human soul, working through the imagination, would be wholly off-limits: Lawrence on blood-sacrifice would have to go, and so would a number of our old classics. We should be left to love one another, and die of boredom.

Most of the passages Mr Harrison quotes from the *Cantos* are neither poetry nor economics nor politics; yet they have considerable interest for the humanist as evidence of one man's sheer indomitability, his refusal to lay down his bow and arrow in a world of nuclear weapons. Pound's anti-semitism is bound to seem wicked now, or at the very least more difficult to account for; the same is true of Eliot's Jewish references. A lot of blood has passed into the soil since then. In this whole matter of fascist flirtation Mr Harrison and the rest of us have the wisdom of hindsight. Mr Harrison remarks justly on Eliot's disgust for 'the mechanics of sex', and notes that

> Sweeney would be a more acceptable symbol of modern sexual degeneration if Eliot gave more convincing examples of sexual success than oblique references to Marvell's *Coy Mistress* and Day's *Parliament of Bees*!

Again, there is a mystery here: though its 'sense' can scarcely be described as life-enhancing, though its references to sex are grotesquely caricatural and its attitude towards the lower orders is supercilious and even callous, yet *The Waste Land* can still generate great excitement in the minds of readers, especially young ones, and in readers whose social and moral views are in no way 'reactionary'. Do we go to literature—or do we go *these days*—chiefly to be castigated, and thereafter to feel better? Does literature perform the function of the *memento mori*, is poetry the death's-head of humanism? Will it always be in opposition to any plan intended to better the lot of mankind, whether democratic or totalitarian? If so, then it will serve a useful purpose: even a democracy (and not unnaturally

Mr Harrison is only concerned with the British experience)
can cast up scoundrels and seat them in power. We put up with
Yeats's 'Marching Songs' (they don't exactly exert an evil
fascination!) for the sake of the nobility, strength, courage and
stoicism which he makes manifest elsewhere, qualities which
we hope are not going to vanish entirely from the face of a
democratic earth.

Artists are obsessed with art, they 'live for it'. And they are
under a powerful temptation to feel, as Mr Harrison puts it,
that 'art does not exist for man, man exists for art, therefore
society must be organised so that the arts will flourish'. In
1927 Wyndham Lewis declared that 'no artist can ever love
democracy . . .'. Further, the artist is conscious of inequality,
more than workers in other fields, forever conscious that one
poem or painting is better or worse than another, one poet or
painter superior or inferior to another. The writer is engaged
in showing his *difference* from other writers, not his similarity
with them. It is not surprising if he fails to remind the reader
frequently enough that there *is* a sense, another sense, in which
all men are equal. Then too, as Erich Heller has pointed out,
the distribution of creative genius over the ages makes nonsense of the idea of progress in the arts. Helped by his daily
paper, the artist is tempted to extend his scepticism into other
spheres of human endeavour.

Though he provides a good deal of not always indispensable
reference to historical writing on the period, Mr Harrison
ignores some critics and philosophers who have explored this
fearfully intricate subject. Lionel Trilling, for one; and Erich
Heller, who (whether or not you agree with his conclusions)
must be admitted to have thought deeply and protractedly
about the relationship between literature and politics. For
instance: 'the poetic imagination is naturally more a glorifier
of memories than a designer of utopias, more loyal to origins
than enamoured of causes, more rooted in the past than allured
by the future'. Or, as Yeats wrote, 'Man is in love and loves
what vanishes.' Mr Harrison makes some mention of Thomas
Mann's early conservatism, but doesn't deal with his later
history; nor does he look at that mysterious early remark of
Mann's in the *Meditations of a Non-Political Man* (1918):

Why all this labour? Why the prolonged and humiliating servitude in which I am kept by this book? . . . Could it be that what I am . . . does not correspond exactly to what I think and believe, and that I am destined to further precisely that which on these pages I have called 'Progress' through the very act of conservatively opposing it—opposing it by means of 'literature'?

Not notably a piece of 'clear thinking', one would say! And perhaps Mr Harrison's unwillingness to descend into mystery comes out in his reference to 'a man of letters, or any other clear thinker . . .'.

If some of the points I have touched on seem intended as extenuation which Mr Harrison might well decline to accept, nevertheless they are points which he should have looked into. His rather literal-minded approach to imaginative writing robs his book of some of the weight it should rightly carry. If you are going to spit in church, you should carry out the operation with thoroughness and conviction. There is not much danger these days of our resorting to literature as some sort of Kruschen Salts or chest-expander. But I don't believe that in our time literature can only be made out of the negative emotions. Mr Harrison's theme is well worth pursuing, and he might turn his attention to later writers, who are able to depress the mind much more efficiently than *The Waste Land* and without exciting the nerves or extending the sensibility. There are parts of the world where people are able to starve with a greater fortitude, even with more cheerfulness, than European and American writers manage to summon up when contemplating the human lot from a comfortable chair. (1966)

III

WISE HEADS, WISE TALES

THE wisdom of the East is at times obscured by the mystery of the East—or, it could be, sustained by it. This phenomenon may help to account for the current popularity of selected snippets from Eastern philosophy, as also of selected techniques from Eastern poetry, at a time when logic, reason and reasonableness are considered to have proved incompetent or corrupt. (As a selected Western snippet has it, a bad workman quarrels with his tools. . . .)

An important variant of the apophthegm is the analogy or parable, much employed by Eastern philosophers. And that a thinker so little metaphysical as Confucius should have attracted such masses of commentary might be held to indicate the weakness of this form of teaching. Yet it could also be claimed that discussion is of the essence and the fact that Confucianism survived so long indicates the strength or aptness of the system. People like to be told stories, they like it all the more if there is a suggestion that wisdom lurks somewhere in the story, and often they don't mind much if they fail to detect the wisdom with any certainty.

But we have already committed at least two major sins, in talking of 'Eastern philosophy' as if all philosophies originating in the East were identical, and in implying that all 'Eastern philosophers' were out to teach Truth or the Way of arriving at it all the time and to all comers. The second, at least, of these sins we had better attempt to expiate. Unfortunately, there is an evasiveness which betokens a breakdown in thinking either accidental or prudential and an evasiveness which is intended to leave the door open for the pupil to make his own way through. On top of that, there are times when we personally welcome evasiveness and other times when it irritates us: one's reception of Eastern wisdom would seem to lie more at the mercy of one's state of mind than such things (but think of Shakespeare interpretation!) ought to. But there too the sages cover themselves. They tell us, or some of them do, that the provoking of irritation is itself one technique of teaching: make a man mad and you may possibly make him wise. Thus the Sufis have gone out of their way to annoy and antagonise, to court blame and abuse, in order to make a point. Idries Shah describes this as the high form to which masochism or 'holy suffering' is the corresponding low and degenerate form, and their deliberate clowning is thus akin to the more austere riddling of the Zen masters (though the latter can be coarse: 'What is the Buddha?' 'A dry shitstick'). If, however, the 'irritation' doesn't work in this way and the recipient is merely repelled, then never mind, another useful function has been served: it demonstrates that the pupil would never be able to benefit from instruction. Heads, I have taught you; tails, you are unteachable. It seems as if the sages can never lose.

For one thing, it is a mistake to suppose that these teachers are necessarily intent on teaching. 'You cannot,' as some wise man has said, 'make a silk purse out of a sow's ear.' And to judge from the stories in Idries Shah's collection, *The Dermis Probe*, the Sufis arrived at a mode of selection which puts all academic Boards of Admissions to shame. In his earlier book, *The Sufis*, he quoted this interchange between a would-be pupil and a teacher: 'I wish to learn, will you teach me?' 'I do not feel that you know how to learn.' 'Can you teach me how to learn?' 'Can you learn how to let me teach?' How many academics would dare to inaugurate their tutorials in such a way—even given the opening? Incidentally, students prone to study the criticisms rather than the texts might profit from the Sufi saying that you cannot send a kiss by messenger.

Though plainly very different in demeanour, Mencius remarked, somewhat ambiguously but with that air of cool, slightly pained superiority which generally accompanies him, at any rate in English translation: 'There are more ways than one of instructing others. My disdain to instruct a man is itself one way of instructing him.' It is a way which does not recommend itself in the West, where there have usually been more people ready to teach than to learn—unlike the East, where people are keener to improve themselves than to improve others, or so one would have said had not Mencius also remarked, 'The trouble with people is that they are too eager to assume the role of teacher'.

One thing we notice about many Sufi apophthegms is that they can be reversed and still make sense. 'The mine is always bigger than the gem'—why not 'the gem is always bigger than the mine'? 'If you cannot lie down, you will stand up once too often': very true, but reversed it is even better—'If you cannot stand up, you will lie down once too often.' Then there are the permutations on 'One lie will keep out forty truths'—'Forty lies will keep out one truth'. 'One truth will keep out forty lies' (a little sanguine perhaps, or unctuous, but philosophers generally have their moments of high-minded sentimentality), 'Forty truths will keep out one lie'—each of which at least provokes a little thought, and the thinking will not be of an abstract kind but rather turned towards actual human situations —and 'he who tastes, knows'.

Proverbs are not meant to *solve* problems, and a Sufi proverb has it that 'a solved problem is as useful to a man's mind as a broken sword on a battlefield'. One advantage claimed for the use of analogy or allegory is that these devices avoid specific-ness of message: if the teacher is specific in his answer, then 'he would cease to provoke thought and discussion'—in fact he would have put an end to thinking. The tigers of bafflement are wiser than the horses of instruction. Of course this argu-ment can be advanced to justify sheer nonsense or wanton mystification, but as Dryden pointed out, that blank verse can be written badly is not an objection to blank verse. Never-theless some unhappiness is bound to linger. Idries Shah has said, of the amusing stories of Mulla Nasrudin, that one ex-tracts from them only a very little more than one puts into them. Should we feel content if this were proposed as a recom-mendation of poetry? But perhaps we are now mixing genres, and one law for the lion and ox is oppression?

One of the Nasrudin stories tells how the Mulla entered an ox in a horse race. When bystanders laughed at him, he ex-plained that as a calf it ran around very nimbly, so now it was fully grown it would surely run even faster. The story is amenable to several interpretations, one of which is that the logical extension of observed fact can lead us right away from reality—there is indeed more than one law. Here the Mulla is playing the fool in the hope of making his wiser listeners even wiser. One cannot imagine Confucius or Mencius lifting up their robes in this undignified manner—they are unlikely to enjoy the favour of the young if only because of their un-equivocal emphasis on filiality—but for them too analogy was an important mode of exposition and communication.

Mencius's analogies are sometimes rather elusive, as if a factor in the comparison had been omitted, and there is no apparent suggestion that the elusiveness is meant to have a special efficacy. Ch'un-yü K'un opens a session by remarking that, although according to the rites a man and a woman should not touch each other, it would surely be in order to stretch out a hand to save one's sister-in-law from drowning. He then asks Mencius, 'Now the Empire is drowning, why do you not help it?' Mencius replies, 'When the Empire is drown-ing, one helps it with the Way; when a sister-in-law is drown-ing, one helps her with one's hand. Would you have me help the Empire with my hand?' Arthur Waley has described this reply as 'at the best a very cheap debating point'—a mis-carriage or abuse of analogy. However D. C. Lau defends Mencius by explicating thus: in using a hand to save a sister-in-law one is compromising, but the outcome is successful, one does save the lady; if one offers a watered-down version of the Way to a ruler one is compromising, and the outcome will be unsuccessful, because a watered-down Way is not the Way.[1] In support Mr Lau adduces Mencius's statement, 'What can one do about those who bend the Way in order to please others? There has never been a man who could straighten others by bending himself.' But Mr Lau takes it that a pro-nounced dilution of the Way, consequent upon association with unsavoury characters, would be involved, while Waley supposed the interrogator merely to be suggesting that in the present emergency Mencius ought to put aside the 'general principles' which made him hesitate to take office. From the passage itself it is not at all clear what is holding Mencius back, and we might be tempted to see his reply—'Would you have me help the Empire with my hand?'—as the sort of exasperated

[1] *Mencius*, translated with an introduction by D. C. Lau.

rejoinder anyone could make to a person who solemnly asked him why he wasn't bestirring himself to save civilisation.

Moreover, the absolutism implied by Mr Lau's reading doesn't seem to accord with the moderation of Confucian thought. Mencius said, 'Confucius was a man who never went beyond reasonable limits'; and one should avoid extremes even to the point of avoiding extreme moderation: 'Holding on to the middle is closer to being right, but to do this without the proper measure is no different from holding to one extreme. The reason for disliking those who hold to one extreme is that they cripple the Way. . . .' We could do with a few stories to help us sort this proposition out! But elsewhere Mencius tells us that Confucius was ready to give his employers a fair trial; sometimes he took office 'because he thought there was a possibility of practising the Way', sometimes because he had been treated with decency and sometimes because the prince wished to keep good people at his court.

A cryptic exchange which Mr Lau doesn't discuss consists of the question, 'Why did Confucius always take a present with him when he left for another state?' and Mencius's answer, 'A Gentleman takes office as a farmer cultivates land. Does a farmer leave his farming tools behind just because he is leaving for another state?' For if the giving of presents to lords whose service one hoped to enter was an approved custom and totally above suspicion, then why was the question asked? And if there were any doubts about its propriety in the case of a person like Confucius, then surely a more cogent answer is required than this uneasy analogy between Gentleman and farmer, presents and tools?

More plainly unpersuasive, at least to the Western mind, is the assertion that just as clear water is put to a higher use (washing the chin-strap) and muddy water to a lower use (washing the feet)—that is, the water brings the difference in treatment upon itself—so 'only when a man invites insult will others insult him' (well, yes, Christ invited insult) and 'only when a state invites invasion will others invade it'. Associated with this is the proposition that once he appears the good ruler inevitably attracts subjects from all over the Empire by winning their hearts, the people turn to him by the operation of a

M

natural law, 'like water flowing downwards with a tremendous force. Who can stop it?' We might smile at such simplicity, if it didn't remind us of the Mao-Marxist contention that socialism is to replace capitalism in obedience to an objective law whereby all dissident elements are rendered paper tigers.

In any case, Mr Lau is of the opinion that 'an analogy is at least as instructive, if not more, when it breaks down as when it holds'—so, once again, the sage can never lose. And Mencius's advice on how to read the *Odes*—'one should not allow the words to obscure the sentence, nor the sentence to obscure the intended meaning. The right way is to meet the intention of the poet with sympathetic understanding'—is akin to Idries Shah's comment that one doesn't get much more out of a Nasrudin tale than one puts into it.

Our discontent with these elusive and uncertain modes of conveying or eliciting wisdom may be modified if we consider the patchy record of direct and unequivocal instruction. For instance, 'Thou shalt not kill'. In the West we have tended to think that by reasoning we can bring a man to believe something he didn't believe before, even should it deny what he has believed hitherto. Easterners, by and large of course, feel that only the teachable can be taught, that 'good will' in the student is a *sine qua non*, that motivation is all-important (*why* do you want to learn?), that the teacher liberates what is already in the pupil—or else fails to teach. Considering the nature of Maoist techniques, considering also the nature of the Chinese (in particular their hard-headedness, their scepticism on the subject of grand causes, which on occasion could be more sympathetically described as spiritual modesty), Mao might seem to be something of a Westerner. But no, he must be an Easterner, we must suppose he appeals to something in the Chinese past and to something in the Chinese character—perhaps their preference for economical apoththegms and parables which relieve them of the burden of abstract speculation and liberate them for the hard task of staying alive and procreating. (1970)

HEIAN JANE

PEOPLE who complain that Jane Austen's books have little
to do with 'life' ought to be made to study the literature of
the Heian period, of the aristocratic world of tenth-century
Japan. Admittedly Heian society, as we know of it through
the prose writings of its ladies, did go in for sex, but rather
as an exquisite exercise in social manners than as anything
spiritually more momentous for better or worse. To a large
extent, it seems to have been a question of skilfully calculated
risk, of knowing how much to let other people know about
and how much not to. The 'next-morning letter' which the
lover was obliged to send his mistress appears to have loomed
larger than whatever happened the night before. The Japanese
were—are?—an incorrigibly literary people.

Miss Austen admits farmers to the human race. On her way
to the Kamo Shrines one day, Miss Shōnagon[1] observes some
oddly dressed women moving backwards across a field, bending down and then straightening up again—'for what purpose
I cannot imagine'. Ivan Morris comments that the occupation
of planting rice, a common sight, was 'one that no elegant
Court Lady would admit to recognising'—just as once our
ladies could not admit to recognising certain words used by
our gentlemen. Moreover, Shōnagon disapproves of these
particular peasants because they are singing a disrespectful song
about the *hototogisu*, a poetic bird and hence the property of
the upper classes. No nonsense about folk culture here. We
notice, however, that a little later on Shōnagon is less coy when
it comes to recognising the operation of harvesting the rice.
But perhaps consistency was regarded as boring and vulgar.
Among 'Things That People Despise' she includes 'Someone
with an excessive reputation for goodness'.

The common people are referred to here by such polite
circumlocutions—though this one may be literally true—as 'the

[1] *The Pillow Book of Sei Shōnagon*, translated and edited by Ivan Morris.

people of whom one does not know how to speak'. And in a list of 'Unsuitable Things' Shōnagon mentions 'Snow on the houses of common people,' adding that 'This is especially regrettable when the moonlight shines down on it.' And probably, in our day, we do need Professor Morris's gloss: 'Because such beauty is wasted on *hoi polloi* and inappropriate to their gross nature'. There were no working-class poets at that time, no scholarship-boy scholars.

Shōnagon herself was quite a poet, though Professor Morris remarks that her poems are often more ingenious than poetic— an observation which, I would think, applies to a lot of Japanese poetry of whatever date. She is sensitive in all the proper respects and insensitive in the proper respects too. Thus she finds the 'parasite tree' moving or pathetic because it is dependent for its existence on other trees. But when a rather common fellow whose house has burnt down in a fire originating in the Imperial Stables comes to the palace hoping for alms, Shōnagon presents him with a peculiarly obscure and unfeeling poem, thus winning the admiring laughter of her companions, including the Empress. The scheme of priorities and the compartmentation of the sensibility seem, if I may say so, not un-Japanese.

Of course it would be useless to reproach Shōnagon for her undemocratic attitudes. It is equally silly to admire her for them, since they were merely inherited. The highly ritualistic Heian civilisation represented in Shōnagon's journals and (more romantically, Arthur Waley has suggested, and less accurately) in Lady Murasaki's novel, *The Tale of Genji*, will have a special appeal for the modern reader—how Shōnagon would hate to think she was read by us common readers!—and is likely to be over-estimated. Though not, it would seem, by the more sceptical scholars. Professor Morris's comments are sometimes quite tart, albeit expressed in rather gingerly fashion, as if he feared Shōnagon might materialise in his study and stab him with a double-edged quotation, while Waley (who translated about a quarter of *The Pillow Book*, interspersing it with his own commentary) remarked that the 'figures and appurtenances' of the period sometimes seem to us 'to be cut out of thin, transparent paper'. Stretches of *The Pillow Book* are plain

boring, and could have been composed by some lady-in-
waiting of our own day or yesterday—'everything about well-
born people delights me'—though she would need to be a
lady with a sharp visual sense besides a gift for writing fashion
notes.

But neither is this the whole story. Shōnagon was not herself
of especially elevated birth (though a distinguished poet, her
father was also a provincial governor, a class of people not
highly regarded at court), and it seems probable that she was
not a beauty either. To keep her end up, she was dependent
on her learning (or her reputation for learning), her ready wit
and her ready tongue. 'In this palace one is always sorry when
one has made some inadvertent remark,' whines the Captain
First Secretary, who has just been smartly put down by
Shōnagon in the matter of an inapt poetic allusion. One likes
to think of this sharp-tongued lady keeping the under-
employed and over-dressed courtiers on their toes. It says
something for Heian civilisation that Shōnagon was not rudely
silenced! Within the limits firmly imposed by social assump-
tions which apparently no one questioned seriously, she was
truly what in a hardly covert self-reference she described herself as—'a woman who has quick wits and a mind of her
own'.

Her shrewdness, among other qualities, comes out in one of
the liveliest sections of *The Pillow Book*, on 'Hateful Things',
where, as in most of her catalogues, sentiments to which every
bosom returns an echo rub shoulders with feelings which
strike us as arbitrary and esoteric. On the one hand,

> One is telling a story about old times when someone breaks in
> with a little detail that he happens to know, implying that one's
> own version is inaccurate—disgusting behaviour!

On the other,

> An elderly person warms the palms of his hands over a brazier
> and stretches out the wrinkles. No young man would dream of
> behaving in such a fashion; old people can really be quite shame-
> less.

Then we have this:

> A man with whom one is having an affair keeps singing the
> praises of some woman he used to know. Even if it is a thing of
> the past, this can be very annoying. How much more so if he is
> still seeing the woman! (Yet sometimes I find that it is not as
> unpleasant as all that.)

Fleas too, we hear, are very hateful—we are reminded of
Pope's incongruous juxtapositions in *The Rape of the Lock* ('Or
stain her honour or her new brocade')—'When they dance
about under someone's clothes, they really seem to be lifting
them up.' A little later one is told how 'Sometimes one greatly
dislikes a person for no particular reason—and then that person goes and does something hateful'. Though not exactly a
pleasant one, Shōnagon was certainly a rare character, and
cut out of something much tougher than paper. (1968)

ENOUGH IS AS GOOD
AS AN ORGY

LI YÜ (if Li Yü it was who wrote the novel originally pub-lished in or around 1634 under the title 'The Prayer Mat of Flesh') quite possibly had his tongue in his cheek throughout. His German translator takes it all *au grand sérieux*, although the translation (or rather the English translation of the German translation of the novel which may have been written by Li Yü) displays a saving skittishness on matters and in contexts which only a certain skittishness could save. Be all that as it may (or may have been, in Chinese), Li Yü (or his translator, or his translator's translator) offers us the Apologia for Pornography in what is surely its richest and ripest form.

The moral of *The Before Midnight Scholar*[1] is this: Don't chase skirts. Not that the tendency of the work is against sex. On the contrary. Man's life is full of hardship and grief, so 'let us therefore be thankful to the Creator of heaven and earth for having made two different sexes,' it says on the first page, 'and for providing that there should be relations between them'. But, asks the author, if a man has 'his legitimate spouse at home and, if you will, a collateral wife or two,' then why should he wander abroad and squander his money on strange women? 'What he needs is there at hand; he need only sit down to table.' The author hopes that 'the esteemed reader will not fail to understand the author's kindly, motherly intent'.

The author is a sophisticated man, always several steps ahead of his esteemed if naïve reader. The latter, he remarks, will enquire, 'If your intentions are so moral, my dear author, why have you not just written a treatise about moral reform? Why have you given us instead a spicy novel in which all sorts of "breezy" deviations from good conduct are described minutely?' But Li Yü needs no expert witnesses, come from the univer-sities and the churches, to plead his cause. 'Dear friends,' he

[1] Translated by Richard Martin from the German version by Franz Kuhn.

says calmly, soothingly, 'let me explain.' Such is the depravity
of the times that a very thick coating of sugar is required to
sweeten the pill of morality. 'The present-day reading public
has a positive horror of educational, moralistic books written
in the dry, solemn style of the ancient classics and historians.'
They don't care what Confucius says. Indeed, 'it is no exag-
geration to say that certain parts of our society have today
attained the peak of amorality, not to say laxity and licence'.
So Li Yü adduces glorious instances from the past, of great
emperors and great teachers, who fought fire with fire, water
with water, and won. His present technique (and it is mag-
nanimous of him to tip us off at the outset) is to entice the
esteemed reader along the path of salvation, joyously hurrying
from spicy passage to spicy passage, until all of a sudden, when
he is off his guard, the axe will fall. Then, like the reader of
Swift's *Modest Proposal*, 'he will wake up in terror and say:
"Gracious me! Is that how it is? . . . Better stick to your own
wife and your own collateral wives at home!"' Not long ago
a letter-writer in the *New Statesman* surmised that the sex stuff
in *Hiroshima mon Amour* 'attracted many viewers who might
not otherwise have watched an anti-war film'. Here, however,
the fire of lust is to be driven out by the fire of lust, though Li
Yü prefers to describe this technique as 'conjuring up the
innocent white lotus blossom from swamps and muddy pools'.
He makes our present-day campaigners for the sexual freedom
of the press look like a lot of schoolboys petitioning the headmaster for the return of a confiscated copy of *Men Only*.

   Thus the moral of this story is that if you chase too many
skirts—and catch them—then in the end you may well do
yourself an injury. Just as the hero of the story does himself an
injury in the end, with a vegetable knife. As a precaution, the
moral is enforced at the beginning of the book and at its end.
In between we have the sugar, a fast-moving sequence of
'vernal lusts and aberrations,' comprehending most of the
better-known combinations and permutations, of which it will
suffice to say that the feats are generally credible in kind if not
always in quantity. Some of the material seems to be honestly
didactic and even effectively instructive, among other things,
and the point is pushed home that the object of the exercise is to

give pleasure as well as take it. It is perhaps a pity that the
Scholar should be represented as so poorly endowed by nature
as to require to undergo a highly improbable (and painless)
operation involving the involuntary co-operation of a young
male dog. Animals are otherwise out, and the reader will
appreciate the high standard of social behaviour, for courtesy
and propriety prevail even at the unlikeliest moments. 'When
he attempted the "fetching fire behind the hill" position, she
said it was an offence against decorum to turn one's back on
one's husband.' The concept of sin, of guilt, only exists in the
vicinity of the covers of the book, and even there it is, by
Christian standards, a somewhat remote consideration, a question of regret over some social shortcoming or the deplored
discovery of a deficit in the spiritual accounts. The language
is elegant, since the customary elegance of gallant literature is
heightened by the customary elegance of Chinese (or of
Chinese-literally-translated). 'His noble yak whisk will pene-
trate her pleasure grotto without difficulty. . . .' 'With his last
strength he pressed his nephrite proboscis into the sanctum of
her flower-temple.' Or, a nice addition to our limited reper-
toire, 'her breasts felt like freshly laid hen's eggs without shells'.
Or, of a not very amazing practice, 'the technical term . . . is "to
coax the source into flowing by removing the pebbles".'
Actually the expertise is largely in the linguistic field: instead
of four-letter words we are offered complete poems.

Few of the characters in *The Before Midnight Scholar* are at all
interesting by virtue of what they are as distinct from what
they do, though there is a nice wise cat-burglar with high
ethical principles, who is able to report expertly on varieties of
sexual behaviour as observed more or less reluctantly by an
innocent bystander eager to be about his proper business. The
women vary only in degrees of beauty and of social standing
or lying, and in a few other details whose variousness enables
our Scholar to demonstrate the exactness of his scholarship.
To the Western mind there will seem to be a good deal more
calculation in evidence than passion, though the latter is by no
means absent. The Chinese lover, like Messrs Amis and Con-
quest's character in *The Egyptologists*, is not given to disar-
ranging hair-do's or tearing blouses, but is content to forfeit

'the quite valuable effect of ungovernable passion attributable to
such excesses'. The Chinese head and the Chinese heart are
never altogether divorced, it might seem; and even their love-
suicides tend to have an element of the ritualistic about them,
planned and methodical albeit artistic. No dissociation of sensibility here. Thus our hot-blooded hero takes a room in a
temple much frequented by young women (it is dedicated to
the deity Chang, 'the bestower of children'), and scouts for
local talent from a vantage point behind the god's broad back.
He compiles a short-list of favoured candidates entitled 'Vernal
apparitions from far and wide' in which he includes such
personal data as name, age, single or married, and

> in addition he would mark the names with little cinnabar red
> circles just as a high examiner marks the examination papers of
> the candidates, and group them according to quality. One red
> circle next to a name meant 'average', two red circles meant
> 'very good', and three 'outstanding'. After name and description
> there would be a brief description of the candidate's advantages.

We are much nearer to Lamb's 'Utopia of gallantry' here than
we ever are in the world of the Restoration comedians.

Her husband having left her in search of adventure, the
Scholar's wife consoles herself with 'erotic novels of dubious
quality'. The accounts therein bear no resemblance to reality,
judging by the reality of her husband as she knew him—that is,
before canine reinforcement. It is a measure of Li Yü's sophisti-
cation, if not his humorousness, that she should tell herself,
'You mustn't believe everything you read in books. . . . Surely
the miraculous items described in these pornographic books
are pure invention, products of the author's imagination. . . '.
And later, spying on a creditable performance in her maid's
bedroom, she remarks, 'What vigour, what endurance! . . .
It was just like a novel.' The Golden Casket[1] contains a story
called 'The Peony Lantern', about a young man who falls in
love with the ghost of an unsatisfied girl who soon drives him

[1] Chinese Novellas of Two Millennia, translated by Christopher Levenson
from Wolfgang Bauer's and Herbert Franke's German version of the
original Chinese.

into her grave. The two spirits then haunt the town, till a wise Taoist persuades the bailiffs in the Beyond to arrest them as a public nuisance. After a good whipping the ghosts confess their sins. 'I acted contrary to warnings against lust,' says the young man, 'and was infected by excessive sensual desires.' The girl confesses that, though her soul had left her body, 'my vital urges were not yet quite extinguished,' and so she had returned to earth where she found 'a lover with whom I could have enjoyed five hundred years of mutual bliss and offered countless thousands of people material for lustful stories.' Or, of course, for moral ones.

One other story in this collection is of the erotic genre, re-calling the novel, *Chin P'ing Mei* ('The Golden Lotus'): 'The Emperor and the Two Sisters', written, we are told, about the time of Christ's birth, in which the Emperor dies horribly from an overdose of an aphrodisiac called 'Prudence-saving Glue'. Love interest of one sort or another is never far away in *The Golden Casket*, but the fantastic stories are probably the best, foremost among them 'A Lifetime in a Dream' (late eighth century) and 'The Island of the Black Coats' (twelfth century), the first recounting a sojourn in the country of the ants, finely and movingly worked out, the second a voyage to the land of the swallows, and both qualifying, I should think, as early examples of science fiction. Perhaps fantasy is a universal con-stant; at all events these tales (and similar Japanese ones) are close to European fairy tales: the rituals and ceremonies, per-haps for oriental writers the least fantastic element in the stories, are readily assimilated to the rituals and ceremonies of Western tales and legends.

Returning to *The Before Midnight Scholar*, we should note that the story is neatly bound, fore and aft, not only by earnest or earnest-seeming moralising but also by the figure of the venerable monk, Lonely Summit. At the beginning Lonely Summit tells the Scholar that he has the makings of a saint. 'But not yet,' is the young man's answer. The way of the trans-gressor is hard, the monk warns him, and this even-handed justice tends to commend the ingredients of our poisoned chalice to our own lips. But the Scholar argues that even if a gallant were punished by having his wife seduced—or even both wives or all three—he would still come out on top, since he must surely have seduced a far greater number of other men's wives and daughters. The punishment couldn't possibly be made to fit the crime. . . . Towards the end of his adventures the Scholar visits a celebrated courtesan who runs away as soon as she spots him. Pursued to her boudoir by the impetuous Scholar (who has paid a deposit on her), she hangs herself. In their fury—'it was possible that they were even more upset than if their own legitimate spouses had passed away'—the other customers beat up the Scholar. When he recovers his wits he recognises the dead woman as his wife. She had been seduced and then sold into a brothel. 'Now I am brought face to face with the bitter truth: whereas I fornicated with a mere six women, my own wife seems to have done so with hundreds of men—with several dozen at the very least.' This unhappy piece of arithmetic serves to convert him to a religious life: 'the hour of repentance and meditation has come.' Changing his name to 'Stupid Pebble', he attaches himself as a novice to Lonely Summit. It only remains for him to rid himself of that part of him which is partly of canine origin and thus 'highly displeasing to Buddha', and this he does successfully, and even (once again) painlessly.

Moralising aside, it must be admitted that, in respect of everyday life in the China of the time (as distinct from every-night life), *The Before Midnight Scholar* is nowhere near as informative as *Chin P'ing Mei*, 'the great novel of manners' as Dr Franz Kuhn terms it, which preceded it by some seventy years. In comparing the two works, Dr Kuhn observes that they are alike in respect of the number of women involved: Hsi-men has a main wife and five collaterals, while the Before Midnight Scholar has a main wife, one collateral, and four lady friends. Ethically Dr Kuhn seems to give *The Before Midnight Scholar* the edge over the *Chin P'ing Mei*, telling us that 'if there is still the slightest doubt as to the author's good intentions . . . it should be dispelled by the highly informative preface to the Japanese edition (B) of 1705'. What this preface tells us is that the owner of the *Tu ch'ing-shu ssu*, 'Publishing House for Erotica', was desirous to publish the novel in Japanese 'and so do his bit toward reforming the unscrupulous libertines, the light-minded seducers' of Japan,

who neglect their own wives and collateral wives, while flinging
themselves into gallant adventures with strange women, going so
far as to climb walls and bore their way through partitions for the
sole purpose of arriving at the goal of their shameless desires . . .
Then we shall have a harmonious family life and orderly conditions
in our country—that is the moral, that is the wonderful guiding
idea of this novel . . .

Well, Dr Kuhn is the scholar.

At all events, compared with the enseamèd beds and nasty
stics of current Western fiction, *The Before Midnight Scholar*
undeniably has its refreshing and even its sensible side. 'If your
nose offends you,' it says in effect, 'then cut it off.' A misprint
at the very end of the novel—or perhaps it isn't a misprint?—
provides us with the timeliest moral of all:

> From this it can be seen that everyone in this world can aspire to
> Buddhahood. It is only wordly desires which shackle them, and
> prevent them from escaping from the vanity of the world and
> reaching salvation on the other side.

True, alas, the word (four-letter or cognate) is too much with
us, late and soon, getting and spending. . . . (1965)

THE JAPANESE NOBEL

IN the course of a recent tutorial on *Paradise Lost* I was reminded by a Chinese nun that we were not talking about God but only about Milton's God. I must make it quite clear that I am now talking not about Kawabata but only about Edward G. Seidensticker's Kawabata.

We gather that, while they were gratified by the award of the Nobel Prize to one of their authors, the Japanese intelligentsia were surprised that it should go to Yasunari Kawabata. It may be that the Japanese doubt whether Westerners are racially capable of appreciating a writer so famously delicate and 'Japanese' as this one. Or, less hurtfully, they may feel that a writer so sensitive, so allusive and so 'Japanese' as Kawabata cannot translate very meaningfully into another language. Or they may simply be surprised that the award was made to Kawabata rather than to some other Japanese writer. (Quite possibly some of them would have felt happier had a writer less firmly traditional and more up to date been chosen.)

Personally, as a rather removed and entirely lay observer of the Japanese scene, I am rather surprised that the prize was not awarded to Junichirō Tanizaki, who died a few years ago. Tanizaki has written some rather frightful stuff of a kind one cannot imagine ever oozing from the fastidious pen of Kawabata—I am thinking of *Diary of a Mad Old Man* and *The Key*, works which scarcely show that 'idealistic tendency' desiderated by the Founder—but he has also produced work which is simultaneously 'Japanese' *and* accessible to a reasonably wide foreign public. The novels, *Some Prefer Nettles* and *The Makioka Sisters*, and the stories collected under the title *Seven Japanese Tales*: this is writing which I should say, judging by the translations, is much more varied in range and considerably more powerful in impact than the translated works of Kawabata. But this may be my Western bad taste flaunting itself.

Kawabata's two translated novels have now been reprinted in one volume under the rubric, the Nobel Prize Edition.[1] *Thousand Cranes* (understandably the second to be translated into English) is the later of the two, written in 1954/55, whereas *Snow Country* was written between 1934 and 1947. *Thousand Cranes* would certainly be a hot contender for the No-tell Prize, since the most attentive reader, and the most prurient, will be hard put to it to know what exactly is going on at times. The 'story' concerns the relations of a young man with two of his late father's mistresses—but these crude European terms are probably quite inapt here, 'relations' and 'mistresses' in especial!—and with the legitimate daughter of one of those old mistresses. Where the book comes alive is when the characters are talking about tea-ceremony bowls and other ritual accessories. Symbols are they? But why bring in symbols to express what elsewhere you are carefully suppressing?

Does one's recognition of the sensitiveness of the writing prohibit one from complaining that the characters are so faintly drawn as to seem hardly two-dimensional even? I suspect that the occasional awkwardness of the translation here, as compared with the overt skill of the same translator in *Snow Country*, is less an indication that the translator has taken on more than he can manage than that there is simply less to manage. The heart of the novel—and it beats feebly—seems to lie in a confusion of persons. Mrs Ota (did she have to be referred to as Mrs Ota all the time, even in the thoughts of her daughter and her lover?) confuses the young man with his dead father, and then the young man confuses Mrs Ota's daughter with the dead Mrs Ota.

> A jar that had been Mrs Ota's was now being used by Chikako. After Mrs Ota's death, it had passed to her daughter, and from Fumiko it had come to Kikuji.
>
> It had had a strange career. But perhaps the strangeness was natural to tea vessels.

[1] Three of his stories are available in English too: 'The Izu Dancer', in *Perspective of Japan*, *The Atlantic*, 1954; 'The Mole', in *Modern Japanese Literature*, edited by Donald Keene, 1956; and 'The Moon on the Water', in *Modern Japanese Stories*, edited by Ivan Morris, 1961.

In the three or four hundred years before it became the property of Mrs Ota, it had passed through the hands of people with what strange careers?

The tea bowls last longer (and, one feels, burn brighter) than any of the persons—except for one bowl which is broken, perhaps symbolically.

'Had the breach in her cleanness rescued him? There had been no resistance from Fumiko, only from the cleanness itself.' Finally it might appear that the young man makes love with the daughter—or maybe not. Depending upon how you interpret the girl's breaking of the bowl and the laconic reference to her possible shame. But when the characters don't know why they do what they do or feel how they feel, it is hardly up to us to pronounce on what they do or how they do it. The ending is quietly cryptic, and that is all. A Chinese reader whose opinion I solicited declared that the story left us with grave suspicions—a highly unsatisfactory state of affairs! And if I might venture a racial generalisation—bad taste though it be to do so—I would suggest that on the whole the Chinese prefer to know what is being done and who is doing it to whom, whereas by comparison the Japanese are willing to be unsure. Such ignorance, or rather non-knowing, is not exactly to be described as bliss, but seems to be regarded as a spiritual or aesthetic condition distinctly superior to ordinary wisdom.

Snow Country is distinctly superior to *Thousand Cranes*, I should think. If Kawabata is to be prized as a psychologist and more particularly for his female psychology, then there is more interesting psychology and more particularly female psychology to be found here. If he is to be prized as a stylist, as a prose writer in the tradition of *haiku* (those open-ended poemlets), then there are more *haiku* and more interesting ones to be found here. The plot is thin, even emaciated, and concerns a love affair (though 'love' is not quite the word, nor is 'affair') between a dilettante from Tokyo and a hot-spring geisha. Shimamura is an 'idler who had inherited his money', and he writes about Western ballet without ever having seen any:

Nothing could be more comfortable than writing about the ballet from books. A ballet he had never seen was an art in another world. It was an unrivalled armchair reverie, a lyric from some paradise. He called his work research, but it was actually free, uncontrolled fantasy. He preferred not to savour the ballet in the flesh; rather he savoured the phantasms of his own dancing imagination, called up by Western books and pictures. It was like being in love with someone he had never seen.

Komako, the geisha, chats happily about movies and plays she has never seen, either:

Her manner was as though she were talking of a distant foreign literature. There was something lonely, something sad in it, something that rather suggested a beggar who has lost all desire. It occurred to Shimamura that his own distant fantasy on the occidental ballet, built up from words and photographs in foreign books, was not in its way dissimilar.

And it was possible, we are told, that while 'hardly knowing it,' Shimamura 'was treating the woman exactly as he treated the occidental dance'.

Shimamura is cold, relentlessly conscious, and sterile, an aptly wan portrait of an uncreative aesthete, a quite unsatirical portrait, for Shimamura recognises himself for what he is:

He stood gazing at his own coldness, so to speak . . . All of Komako came to him, but it seemed that nothing went out from him to her. He heard in his chest, like snow piling up, the sound of Komako, an echo beating against empty walls.

Komako is a mixture of passion and resignation; she is able to give herself, but alas there is no one to receive her. Yet perhaps the most vivid presence in this novel is that of the snow country itself. Sensitively and adroitly as Kawabata conveys sensuality in inter-human relationships, the relationship between humans and nature is more strongly and more interestingly sensual here—as in *Thousand Cranes*, it may seem, is the relationship between humans and art objects. Human effort goes to waste,

N

men and women are like the dew which soon dries up and vanishes, but the snow country endures. This novel ends—or open-ends—as cryptically as *Thousand Cranes*, but on a firmer note. Though Shimamura is nothing, Komako, usefully or not, is something, is alive. She is probably one of the best, most engaging, most touching, female portraits in Japanese fiction —outside that written by Japanese women.

An odd choice for the prime international award? Kawabata has been Chairman of the Japan P.E.N. Club for many years, and active as critic and editor and in fostering young talent. All this, I imagine, was weighed by the Nobel Prize Committee, along with advice from Japanese scholars and scholars of Japanese on the subject of his creative work. It is right that the Prize should go to Japan, that enormously literary country, and it is a blessing that it wasn't bestowed on some bright young knocker-out of pretentious pornography. (1969)

MISHIMA'S WAY

HARAKIRI is a vulgar expression, and thus not properly applicable to what happened. On 25 November 1970 Yukio Mishima performed *seppuku* at an Army headquarters in Tokyo. It seems that, together with a group of followers, he proposed to raise a coup against the 'weak' Japanese Government and in favour of rearmament and an enhancement of the spirit of patriotism at present threatened by material prosperity. The Army, officers and men, do not appear to have responded with much enthusiasm. One course of action was left to Mishima, not merely a way out but also a way on. He thrust his sword into his left side and dragged it in prescribed manner across his belly. Honour satisfied, one of his companions struck Mishima's head off. The companion in turn commenced the act of self-disembowelment and another member of the group struck his head off. The snag in this process is that finally someone is left without a friend to despatch him. According to reports, the three remaining samurai gave themselves up.

The first reaction to this news of those who knew something about Mishima must have been incredulity. At 45, Mishima was a fantastically successful and prolific author, his reputation as high and as widespread as any in the world. He had written novels, stories, plays, essays; ten of his fictions had been made into films; he had won all the major Japanese awards and would surely have received the Nobel Prize within a matter of years. He was an actor (but more of that later) and an athlete; he had married in 1958 and had a son and a daughter. Moreover, he had been a hero of youth, a cult figure at home, and internationally the best-known of Japanese writers because apparently the most 'accessible'—though this, I must admit, has always puzzled me. Yet he mounted an attack on the Japanese Army, not for existing, but for not existing with sufficient strength and conviction. And he killed himself in a way which is not only exclusively Japanese but also the end and ultimate of that phenomenon which I can only call Japaneseness.

One's second reaction could well be complete credence. What happened was not all that surprising, for two reasons: Mishima was a Japanese, and Mishima was Mishima. Admittedly, the sexual 'frankness' of his writing may have made us think how Western and how modern he was—in the line of Gide, Miller, even Mailer, even (in his occasional mixing of sex and violence) the Soho porn-shops—and the more so if all we knew of Japanese literature was the *haiku*, that species of verse which is all soul and no body, all refinement and no roughage. His *Five Modern Nō Plays* may have struck us, especially if we were unacquainted with *Nō*, as having something in common with the 'Absurd', though they must also have struck us as rather more interesting than most exercises in that modish mode. As for his concern with the Marquis de Sade—what could be more Western and up to date than that?

In fact, all the time Mishima was intensely Japanese. The determined perversity of *The Temple of the Golden Pavilion*, the fearful consciousness of it all and (to our eyes at least) the final ludicrousness. The young woman squeezing milk out of her breast into an army officer's cup of tea, the hero trampling on the belly of a pregnant prostitute, another character raping a 60-year-old widow who is engaged in worshipping his club-foot. . . . The exquisitely airless study of homosexuality and alienation in the early *Confessions of a Mask*. . . . The attendant horrors of the recently translated *Forbidden Colours*, such as the ageing author who forces a *Nō* mask representing young womanhood against the face of his drowned unfaithful wife, so that her face 'buckled under the mask like so much ripe fruit', or the 43-year-old (and married) Count who 'had been intimate with about a thousand boys' (incidentally, the book's American publisher saw it as 'an attack on oppressive Japanese marriage customs', among other things). . . . Etsuko, the Cold Comfort Farmer of *Thirst for Love*, who kills her lover, the hired man, with a mattock, while living semi-incestuously with her father-in-law; the book asks significantly, 'Is sickness perhaps, after all, only an acceleration of life?' . . . And of course one must not forget the overtly 'traditional' subject-matter of the celebrated story, 'The Priest of Shiga Temple and His Love', or the strongly regional fishing-village idyll of *The Sound of Waves.* . . .

Much of this could be thought of as 'Western' because of the 'extreme' nature of the situations and events, just as the mixture in Mishima's characters of obsessive introspection with gratuitous action could be considered distinctively modern. And yet—as I suggested recently in reviewing an obnoxious novel by a young Japanese whom his American publisher described as 'revolutionary' and 'the first truly modern Japanese writer'—Japanese writers of fiction have been modern in this sense for a long time, and 'extreme situations' are no import from the incontinent West!

I have come to suspect that the more the Japanese 'ape' the West, the more Japanese they become. Earlier I used to think that the sort of Japanese who always wore *kimono* and never Western garb, who didn't read English and spoke it as little as possible, who lived sequestered in Kyoto or Nara and was the world's leading expert in (say) the seventeenth-century chronicler Saikaku (lots of indigenous near-porn there!), who had no truck with the P.E.N. or with cultural emissaries from anywhere at all except conceivably China—I used to think that such men, with their cult of nationalism and their distaste if not abhorrence for the West, were dangerous. Latterly, however, I have wondered whether, by comparison, there wasn't almost a racial quiescence about them, and whether those other Japanese who took so keen and protracted an interest in things foreign and modern didn't actually intensify and exacerbate their nationalism, didn't grow even more self-conscious about their Japaneseness. There is nothing like living in a world, whether of reality or fantasy, which is foreign or semi-foreign to make you feel more like what you are. It is a commonplace that Englishmen living in the East and studying things Eastern have sometimes found themselves becoming consciously 'British' to such a degree that, once home again, they realise that they have approached very near to the verge of caricature.

Japan is a precarious country—oh, not for the foreigner, who is of a different species and fully recognised as such!—a land of delicate balances and nervous tensions, where one extreme can quickly spill into its opposite with no middle resting-place. To take an instance far removed from melodrama: a gathering of literature professors round a table. In order of seniority, each speaks his piece on the subject 'under discussion', and when one finishes all the others nod appreciatively, presumably assentingly. It occurs to the foreign observer that the statements expressed are mutually incompatible, even distinctly contradictory. But everyone has his say, everyone nods, there is no movement to compare opinions, no overt acknowledgement of a disagreement which must be obvious to everybody. The meeting concludes in what appears to be complete amity and mutual satisfaction. I don't mean this is necessarily a bad thing. But the point is that argument would hurl the event from amicability and mutual respect into irrevocable estrangement and disrespect; some of those present would cause face to be lost, others would lose it, and the gentlemen might never be able to look one another in the face again. . . .

Racial generalisations are often odious—but they are difficult to avoid unless you stay put in your native village and refuse to speak to strangers. In simple terms, the Japanese find it enormously hard to relax. Or to relax without practically disintegrating. A harmless-seeming form of release like having a few drinks with your pals might end with one jolly companion insulting another past redress: though happily there is a civilised convention whereby the incident is so completely forgotten by all concerned that it really never happened, they never met in that bar. . . .

One common solvent seems to be wellnigh missing from the Japanese scene: the ready humour which eases human contacts. Things cannot be laughed off. This could be a difference between the Japanese and their 'elder brothers' the Chinese (though I may be wrong, my observation is of the Overseas Chinese, who have usually had to clip their national wings), for the latter possess a sense of humour—and moreover, I suspect, feel at least as much concern for finance as for face. For all their strong family feeling, the Japanese were traditionally prepared to sacrifice family to Emperor. The Chinese—with a less devout attitude towards supreme authority, hitherto at least—perhaps found nothing indubitably higher than the family: and a good family-man will think twice before committing suicide for abstract reasons. There is little humour in Mishima's work, or else what looks like humour soon reveals an aspect of poignancy or grimness.

In a brash if not impertinent book written some fifteen years ago, I proposed that at the bottom of the Japanese 'enigma' (if an enigma is so persistent and consistent and finally, in its manifestations, so predictable, is it still an enigma?) lay this— that the Japanese were not content to be merely human, they aspired (or the opposite as it might turn out) to be gods (or demons). Or else works of art. I wrote then:

> The Japanese may be unique in that their unusually complicated system of behaviour is based not on a recognition of humanity but on a proud and yet pathetic denial of it. . . . The intolerably high standards which they have set for themselves are surely intimately connected with the thread of sudden and desperate violence which runs through their history. Unable to forgive others, they have resorted to assassination; unable to forgive themselves, they have turned to suicide, in its most agonising forms.[1]

'Gods and Works of Art'—my crude aphorism was a convenient summing-up of what must have struck the most casual foreign visitor: that the conventions of social and personal behaviour demand so much from the individual and supply him with comparatively few palliatives, releases or loopholes. The ice is thin, the water below is deep. All too soon the end of the road is reached, and there is no turning back, no compromise permitted. Then the superior spirit must kill himself. Not suicide by shot-gun or gas-oven or sleeping pills— those are for peasants—but by ritual self-disembowelment. Lovers, it is true, resort to their own sweet way, binding the girl's kimono sash round the two of them and leaping together off a cliff—perhaps, to the dismay of the Bureau of Tourism, a celebrated beauty spot. But love is merely human, ungodlike, even unheroic, and lovers may aptly choose a faintly picturesque but distinctly low-class solution to their problem. . . .

[1] *The World of Dew.*

It is characteristic of the Japanese, particularly when they are being consciously Japanese, to make things as difficult as possible for themselves—as gods and works of art should—and to exalt the painful above the painless. Hence the man of honour has no alternative, unless circumstance alone has deprived him of the necessary instruments, but *seppuku*, surely the most difficult method, possibly (and certainly if not managed adroitly) the most painful, undeniably the messiest for those humbler creatures who must clear up afterwards. And possibly, even for us Westerners, the mode richest in diversely symbolic overtones: the dressing up, the farewell message whether written or spoken (according to reports Mishima cried, 'Long live the Emperor!'), the ceremonial sword, the baring of the belly, the bowels sliding out (as if to liberate the soul from the taint of human flesh), blood everywhere.

Possibly Mishima was one of those in whom an intimacy with the literature and the life of the West served to sharpen, intensify and exacerbate his awareness of being a Japanese. Left, Right; Pacifist, Militarist; Internationalist, Nationalist—it is a short step psychologically, it seems, from the one to the other, once a constant degree of fanaticism is given. In the early 1950's Americans in Japan were disturbed by the Leftism so prevalent among intellectuals and in the press. In great part, I would say, this was a natural result of the war, or of the defeat, for if the Right and the Militarists have so disastrously compromised your country's honour, how can you be anything but Left and Pacifist—at least for a time? In the longer run, it seems to me, the attitudes of the political Right are so much closer to those of the Japanese psyche that there is less to be feared from the Left. And of course less to be looked for from the Left.[1] A form of Communism may do for the pragmatic

[1] The terms 'Left' and 'Right' are here even less precise in meaning than usual. 'Nowhere do disparate ideologies rest more comfortably side by side than in the head of a Japanese, and the total effect, of course, is of a raging anti-intellectualism,' wrote Edward Seidensticker in an article on the Japanese student revolt (*Encounter*, June 1970). He added, 'The anti-intellectualism is itself very Japanese. When the Japanese seek to establish what it is that makes them themselves . . . they generally come up with some variant upon the concept of "sincerity", which means a glorification of action after the dictates of one's heart, and a contempt for cogitation. Precisely such an

and patient Chinese, but any such system of government would soon leave the majority of Japanese feeling like spiritual orphans, disinherited of that within them which can lead equally to great good or to great evil.

Perhaps post-war, post-Hiroshima, the Japanese people were at their best. Unhappiness certainly didn't have to be pursued then. No one could help but admire their stoicism in the face of unrelenting distress, and the rareness of complaint even from those who couldn't be held in the least responsible for what had happened. The question sounds disgusting—but what is prosperity doing to them? It might conceivably turn them into human beings, no better than the rest of us. . . . Mishima was originally considered the spokesman for post-war youth, adrift in the Waste Land, and its spiritual problems. At that time the villain of the piece was Japanese Tradition, for traditions had brought the land to madness and then to waste. But 'après-guerre' is now long past, and if the spiritual problems still persist despite everything, isn't that because the only solution is Japanese Tradition? The brilliant young Japanese whom foreigners could really talk with, the darling of American publishers who visited the U.S. as guest of the State Department and *Partisan Review*, yet it seems Mishima knew which way his blood called him. At times the most aesthetic, the most 'decadent' of writers, yet he went in for weight-lifting and *kendo*, he kept fit. He must have known what a thoroughly Japanese end his thoroughly Japanese patriotism could bring him to.

Mishima himself directed and played the main (and only male) role in a film based on a story of his called 'Patriotism'.[1] It concerns a young officer whose friends are involved in an

---

emphasis is basic to the thought of Kobayashi Hideo, the most eminent of modern Japanese critics, and indeed to that of Mishima, best of the younger novelists.'

Four days after Mishima's death, *The Observer* quoted 'a young woman revolutionary' (i.e., on the Left) as saying, 'Mishima used a samurai sword. We carry Molotov cocktails and bamboo spears. Both have the samurai spirit.'

[1] Included in the collection, *Death in Midsummer*, published in England in 1967.

attempted coup in 1936. He surmises that they didn't invite him to join them out of consideration for his recent marriage. The following day he is to march against these friends. He cannot do this, he cannot be disloyal to the Emperor, he cannot accept a situation in which Imperial troops will be fighting against Imperial troops. He writes a farewell note— 'Long live the Imperial Forces'—and places it in the alcove, alongside a scroll inscribed with the characters signifying 'Sincerity'. He performs the act of *seppuku*, and then his wife, who has sat by throughout, forbidden to assist him, thrusts a dagger into her throat.

I note that in a review I described this story as seemingly 'a straightfaced demonstration of the fantastic spiritual ambitiousness, almost arrogance, which has it that nothing in one's life becomes it as much as leaving it, and leaving it as painfully and messily as possible'. Attempting to re-read the story after the news of Mishima's death, I was physically unable to go on. The act of disembowelment occupies more than four pages of description and, to the horrified reader, seemingly four hours of time:

> ... the blade was already cutting shallow and had revealed its naked tip, slippery with blood and grease. But, suddenly stricken by a fit of vomiting, the lieutenant cried out hoarsely. The vomiting made the fierce pain fiercer still, and the stomach, which had thus far remained firm and compact, now abruptly heaved, opening wide its wound, and the entrails burst through, as if the wound too were vomiting. Seemingly ignorant of their master's suffering, the entrails gave an impression of robust health and almost disagreeable vitality as they slipped smoothly out and spilled over into the crotch ... A raw smell filled the room.

Ghastly as the account is, the words which follow it are almost more shocking:

> It would be difficult to imagine a more heroic sight than that of the lieutenant at this moment, as he mustered his strength and flung back his head.

We may have supposed that this is how the wife sees the husband whom she loves so much. But possibly this was how Mishima himself saw the act itself.

The officer in the story had to do the whole job himself. In our perhaps irrelevant Western way we can hope that Mishima, who in accordance with tradition was able to call on the services of a comrade, suffered much less hideously and long.

In a solemn editorial two days later, *The Times* described Mishima's action as 'a shocking intrusion' of the old Japan. 'Who is to say,' it asked quite sensibly, 'what may be its ramifications, touching deeply-buried nerves in all parts of Japanese society?' Yet, it added judiciously, however twisted the gesture seems to our way of thinking, 'Mr Mishima was promoting a conception of honour and an affirmation of values'. Some contemplation of this honour and its requirements has driven me into the arms of Falstaff. 'God keep lead out of me! I need no more weight than mine own bowels.' Finally *The Times* assured the foreign observer that for him 'there is neither cause for alarm nor for sneering'. Who on earth is going to *sneer*? As for alarm—speaking for myself, I am merely appalled and terrified. (1970)

THE SENSIBILITY OF
V. S. NAIPAUL

Who is India?

FEW people these days, it seems, and very few Indians, regard
A Passage to India as conveying an accurate picture of Indian
life or character. 'Good style,' the Indian will admit appreciatively, 'but not India. . . .' And yet no one—and I rashly
include Indians here—seems able to produce a picture of India
which is either superior in its cogency or even notably different in essentials from Forster's. Forster covered himself by ack-
nowledging the impossibility of 'picturing' India—indeed it was
a large part of the point: the book is a 'passage', and a (generally)
gentle study in misconceptions. Aziz's account of the pro-
venance of the water in the tank near Fielding's house assumes
the power of the Mogul emperors to make water flow uphill.
Miss Quested—the well-intentioned tourist makes the guide
the test—accepts everything Aziz says as literally true. 'In her
ignorance, she regarded him as "India", and never surmised
that his outlook was limited and his method inaccurate, and
that no one is India.' So it seems curiously wrong-headed in
the critics to complain that Aziz is 'unrepresentative', or (since
he doesn't try to explain it) that Forster didn't understand
Hinduism. Forster was writing a novel. In *An Area of Darkness*,
V. S. Naipaul, perhaps unhappily, is not.

The incident of the uphill-flowing water was brought to
mind by Mr Naipaul's Kashmiri engineer. 'That?' he says,
waving his hand at Akbar's late-sixteenth-century fort. 'That
is five thousand years old.' Mr Naipaul's stories are bound to
remind other travellers of similar experiences of their own.
Himself a Trinidad Indian who has spent much of his time in
England, he remarks that the Indian army officer 'even manages
to look English: his gait and bearing are English; his manner-
isms, his tastes in drink are English; his slang is English'. Yes indeed. Several years ago I found myself in a small British party

who were being conducted round Fort William in Calcutta. This treat had kindly (and perhaps not inappropriately) been arranged by the British Council, though my own feeling was that I hadn't come to India to be marched round an army camp, and only the intimation that we should eventually be offered a chota peg or so in the officers' mess dissuaded me from a sick headache. The brisk Indian major pointed out with professional pride how spendidly the fort was placed for shooting down rioters on the main streets. Endeavouring to repel the suspicion that he had actually said 'shooting down the natives', I lagged behind, and hoped to catch sight of something specifically Indian, or at least something less specifically military. The major had taken note of my insubordinate attitude, and as I caught up with the party, 'But *you* can't be British,' he told me sternly. 'I would say that you are French.' No drink was offered. I seem to recall, though, that we were shown the regimental silver.

Perhaps the writer can get nearer to the spirit of a country, or its spirits, in the medium of fiction or poetry, with the help of a free-ranging imagination, than through the head-on collision of an orthodox travel book. Possibly fiction can be truer than non-fiction in spheres where 'the truth' is so enormously hard to come by; paradoxically, a greater objectivity is achieved through poetry or fiction. To write a travel book, which means sticking to the facts in a case where the facts are so many and so diverse, leaves the author dependent on the confrontation of his personality with the small minority of facts which happen to come his way; with the beaten-track or hit-and-run traveller the facts will be merely touristic, and even with the more enterprising or more privileged, they will still be a small minority and inevitably limited in kind by the fact that he *is* a traveller. A travel book by an author of little personality is likely to be plain dull; a travel book by an author with a pronounced personality (like Mr Naipaul) is likely to tell us more about the author than about the country. Heads, the country loses; tails, the author wins.

Mr Naipaul's earlier book on the West Indies hinted pretty strongly at its author's prickly, susceptible nature, the rawness of his nerves, his thinness of skin. In *The Middle Passage* it was the noise, especially in Trinidad, which most obviously tormented him. In *An Area of Darkness* it is the public defecation.

> Indians defecate everywhere. They defecate, mostly, beside the railway tracks. But they also defecate on the beaches; they defecate on the hills; they defecate on the river banks; they defecate on the streets; they never look for cover.

Both books are prone to exasperated generalisation. There, 'History is built around achievement and creation; and nothing was created in the West Indies,' or 'Port of Spain is the noisiest city in the world.' And here, 'To be in Bombay was to be exhausted,' or

> India's strength, her ability to endure, came from the negative principle, her unexamined sense of continuity. It is a principle which, once diluted, loses its virtue. In the concept of Indianness the sense of continuity was bound to be lost. The creative urge failed . . . Shiva has ceased to dance.

Both books are rich in anecdotes, miniature dramas, character sketches, some of them so lively in themselves as hardly to consort well with the prevailing melancholy of the author's conclusions, others, equally vivid, provoking an odd resistance in the reader. The author appears as less than averagely tactful, in small matters at least, and prone to draw into his orbit persons of a disreputable, unbalanced, unhelpable and even violent kind. There are moments in both books when the reader fears that the author (who has a gift for drawing the reader too into his orbit) is about to be badly beaten up. Mr Naipaul loses his temper with an Indian, and then loses his temper with himself for losing his temper. And, such is the author's absorptive power, somehow the reader feels partly to blame for it. His quick exasperation is tied up with his artist's openness and vulnerability, and unhappily in *An Area of Darkness* (a generalising title!) he is mostly open to spectacles of human degradation or double-think or colossal inefficiency. The sight of a beggar, a human ruin, or 'the starved child defecating at the

roadside while the mangy dog waited to eat the excrement',
this arouses pity. But what use is pity?—it soon yields to contempt. Contempt must be fought down—but how, except by
learning to feel nothing? And out of feeling nothing, nothing
can come.

Mr Naipaul agrees with Malcolm Muggeridge (and a number of other Englishmen) that almost the last true Englishmen
are Indians. The epigram flatters neither race. Certainly in his
sense of personal outrage when, say, someone is trying to
cheat him, Mr Naipaul is very much the Englishman, especially
the Englishman during his first few days in the mysterious
East. Except perhaps for its uncommon honesty, this summing-
up of his passage Eastwards could well have come from such a
virginal English traveller.

> After the bazaar of Cairo the bazaar of Karachi was no surprise;
> and *bakshish* was the same in both languages. The change from
> the Mediterranean winter to the sticky high summer of the Red
> Sea had been swift. But other changes had been slower. From
> Athens to Bombay another idea of man had defined itself by
> degrees, a new type of authority and subservience. The physique
> of Europe had melted away first into that of Africa and then,
> through Semitic Arabia, into Aryan Asia. Men had been dimin-
> ished and deformed; they begged and whined. Hysteria had
> been my reaction, and a brutality dictated by a new awareness of
> myself as a whole human being and a determination, touched
> with fear, to remain what I was.

Yes, that terror of annihilation, of losing one's identity, of
dissolving in the great raucous blinding crazy bazaar of un-
humanity—the fear which we try to appease by sweetly calling
it 'home-sickness' .... But the Englishman will never altogether
lose his identity: he is patently, for better or for worse, 'the
Englishman', the effendi, the tuan, the farang, the gaijin, the
foreigner: he will never lose *that* sort of identity. But in India,
as Mr Naipaul points out, Mr Naipaul *looked* like an Indian.

> It was like being denied part of my reality. Again and again I was
> caught. I was faceless. I might sink without a trace into that

Indian crowd. I had been made by Trinidad and England; recognition of my difference was necessary to me. I felt the need to impose myself, and didn't know how.

The determination to remain what he was, to preserve his face, is plain and strong throughout *An Area of Darkness*, and sometimes, I suspect, it prevents him from seeing other people for what they were. 'All things uncomely and broken, all things worn out and old. . . .' Mr Naipaul is something of an aesthete, an aristocrat, he has the sensibility of a brahmin, but not the supporting beliefs—or complacency—or callousness. His puritanical honesty, his refusal to be taken in by talk of Indian spirituality, afflicts him like an ingrowing nail. He is hardly ever out of pain. The reader suffers with him. Perhaps that is all we can do in the face of such colossal suffering—suffer a little ourselves, for a very little it will be, relatively.

The most charming section of the book—the most equable, the most hopeful—is the account of a sojourn in Kashmir, where the miseries and the petty villainies are recounted in greater intimacy of detail and set in a context of humour, patience, everyday life, within the continuity of experience. Though even here public defecation rears its ugly bottom, for once Mr Naipaul has come somewhere near to putting down his roots, he is at peace as nowhere else in the book, his nerves are quiet. God bless Mr Mohd. Sidiq Butt, Proprietor, Liward Hotel, FLUSH SYSTEM. (It was Mr Naipaul who saw to it that the Flush System was removed from its wrappings and actually installed.) While there is much throughout to remind us that he is a novelist, only this—and particularly the inset episode of the brahmin family sightseeing at Awantipur—reminds us that he is the author of *A House for Mr Biswas*. The Sikh with whom he gets so agonisingly entangled would be a splendid creation in a novel: in this context he is bound to be viewed not as a creation, not as an individual, but as a Typical Sikh, Mr Naipaul's Representative of Sikhhood. Similarly the passing reference to 'the fat, impertinent Anglo-Indian girl and the rat-faced Anglo-Indian manager' in his Bombay hotel sounds like a judgement on a whole community, while the history of Rafiq and Laraine, where again Mr Naipaul's novelistic gifts

are used brilliantly, presses itself upon the reader as a parable
about mixed marriage and even, whatever the author's intentions, a rather dreadful warning.

Mr Naipaul expresses himself forcibly and finely on the
subject of caste. You cannot complain that your 'unpalatable
hotel' is dirty, he says, his confessed 'horror of the unclean'
here merging with his moral horror of caste:

> No Indian will agree with you. Four sweepers are in daily atten-
> dance, and it is enough in India that the sweepers attend. They
> are not required to *clean*. That is a subsidiary part of their function,
> which is to *be* sweepers, degraded beings, to go through the
> motions of degradation . . . In Jammu City you will see them
> collecting filth from the streets with their bare hands. This is the
> degradation the society requires of them, and to this they willingly
> submit. They are dirt; they wish to appear as dirt.

From caste he moves to Gandhi, the reformer. Gandhi failed.
That his writings are still immediately relevant to India, like
an up to date guide-book, is the measure of his failure. 'It is
as if, in England, Florence Nightingale had become a saint,
honoured by statues everywhere, her name on every lip; and
the hospitals had remained as she had described them.' The
horror, disgust and anger which India causes in Mr Naipaul are
translated into a gibing at the failed reformer. One can see that
this affords him (and us) a certain relief, but it is surely a little
naïve. Christ failed too, equally obviously. Mussolini succeeded, for the trains ran to schedule. But the world could have
got by without Mussolini, and doubt may be felt as to whether
we could cheerfully have done without Christ. Driven too far,
Mr Naipaul tends to lay about him somewhat indiscriminately.
But I should say he is in the right about the small-time big-
business gurus and their smug and arrogant hangers-on, the
imitation Tagores who make a living out of conscious 'spirituality' or by exploiting cultural caste-aspirations.

He who wrote comfortably of India would not be writing
about India. For the traveller who doesn't manage to keep his
eyes closed possibly it is the most terrifying of countries, posing
the most insoluble of problems. And perhaps the traveller is

o

doomed to a more or less continuous petulance, once he has hardened himself, and petulance itself is a sort of defence. A battered fastidiousness declines into pettiness, a noble indignation into repeated complaints about open sewers. But petulance won't do in a writer. Small things come to loom too large, and some large things get left out of the account. 'Out of all its squalor and human decay, its eruptions of butchery, India produced so many people of grace and beauty, ruled by elaborate courtesy,' Mr Naipaul tells us towards the end of the book.

> Producing too much life, it denied the value of life; yet it permitted a unique human development to so many. Nowhere were people so heightened, rounded and individualistic; nowhere did they offer themselves so fully and with such assurance. To know Indians was to take a delight in people as people; every encounter was an adventure.

It is an honourable attempt to expiate sins of omission, yet it can make little headway against the disease, the brutalisation and the tortured encounters which he has so potently related, in the face of all he means when he says, so harshly, 'It is well that Indians are unable to look at their country directly, for the distress they would see would drive them mad'. The tenor of *An Area of Darkness* is aptly reflected in his conclusion: his Indian journey, he says, 'was a journey that ought not to have been made; it had broken my life into two'. Then ought he to have made a book about the journey? Is this his quiet acknowledgement that the book is not exactly about a journey, a country, but largely about himself, a hybrid production, part novel, with himself as hero, villain, victim and at times clown?

Yet it should be easier for the reader to be generous towards Mr Naipaul's book than it was for Mr Naipaul to be generous about India and the Indians. The book is strongly felt, original, compact and hardly ever dull: which makes it a rarity in its genre. If in the end the reviewer finds himself doubting the fairness of his own comments, perhaps he had better ask himself what sort of a book on India *he* would have written. In this case I am pretty sure of the answer: equally short-tempered, twice as gloomy, and not half as enjoyable. Forster comes to mind again. 'India a nation! What an apotheosis! Last comer to the drab nineteenth-century sisterhood! Waddling in at this hour of the world to take her seat! She, whose only peer was the Holy Roman Empire, she shall rank with Guatemala and Belgium perhaps!' Perhaps as an amenable subject for travel-writers she doesn't yet rank with Guatemala and Belgium. (1964)

A SOUND MAGICIAN IS A
MIGHTY GOD

The Confessions of Aleister Crowley

A FAIR number of years ago I picked up a handsome copy of Conrad's *Heart of Darkness* which, as a note on the fly-leaf proclaimed, bore the (rather spidery) autograph of Aleister Crowley. The price was 10s, marked down to 5s, and then to 2s. This small transaction took place either in my hometown, Leamington, also the birthplace of Crowley, or else in Cambridge, where Crowley too had been an undergraduate, though (happily being moneyed) he was able to leave without a degree, 'like Byron, Shelley, Swinburne and Tennyson'.

The declining market-value of Crowley's autograph indicates the low esteem into which he had fallen before his death in 1947. This 'autohagiography' is unlikely to establish him as anything more than another English Eccentric, *fin de siècle* variety, graded unsuitable for promotion by the British Council. It will not raise his stock in the literary world; as for the arcane world, it is hard to judge, for on the showing of Crowley's confessions this world is as disorderly, mean and shabby as the literary one.

Crowley had no doubts whatsoever about his super-Vincian genius, so at least his autobiography[1] is utterly free from the common vice of self-pity. Apropos of the place of his birth, he tells us in a footnote to the first sentence of Chapter One that 'it has been remarked a strange coincidence that one small county should have given England her two greatest poets— for one must not forget Shakespeare (1550–1616)'. (A further footnote by the editors solemnly rectifies Shakespeare's birth-date.) Yeats, Crowley informs us, was conscious of 'his incomparable inferiority' to Crowley as a poet. He has some sensible if rather brutal things to say about the Celtic revival:

[1] *The Confessions of Aleister Crowley*, edited by John Symonds and Kenneth Grant.

'What is the use of getting up a scarecrow provincialism, in re-establishing a barbarous and fantastic language which is as dead as Gothic and cannot boast sufficient literature to hold the attention of any but a few cloistered scholars—at the price of cutting Ireland off from the main stream of civilisation?' The trouble with Yeats's work was that 'it seemed to me to lack virility'. Crowley's own verse, except when facetious or polemical, is Dowson with a generous dash of sherbet, but it cannot be said to lack virility if for Crowley's 'cuddle' and 'kissable' we substitute, as the context of the quotations invites us to do, the four-letter word and its formations.

Crowley is by no means a figure of fun, and much of this book (though far from all its thousand pages) is extremely readable. Besides being many other and different things, he was a bit of a John Bull, a man of common sense and forthright response, with a British contempt for British hypocrisy. He was a tireless and fearless traveller, especially in the East, refusing to avail himself of the advice and assistance customarily proffered by H.M. consuls, and like many other Britons he considered the Mohammedans vastly superior to all other brands of native life. Like many other Britons too, he only began to warm to the Chinese when a mandarin invited him to a banquet, at which 'the opulence of Trimalchio was concealed beneath the refinement of Lucullus and the culture of Horace'. Rather less Britishly, he admired the coolies because their performance proved the harmlessness of opium: 'I timed the men under the worst conditions ... and they did eight miles without a rest in two hours dead. If those men were "physical wrecks from the abuse of opium", I should like to see the animal in his undamaged state!'

The John Bull element comes out in his insistence that what the natives expect and respect is authority—and never mind reasonableness. 'No sooner does the sahib suspect that he is not Almighty God than the attributes of Jehovah cease to arm him with unreasonable omnipotence.' Our prestige in India perished because 'we allowed the intellectual Bengali to invade England and caress our housemaids in the precincts of the Earl's Court exhibition'. Yet his 'imperialism' is wholly *sui generis*, and the only pro-consuls who could possibly have lived up to it would be Sir Richard Burton, one of his few heroes, and (his chief hero) himself. He speaks pungently against the Victorian age and the sentimental view of it which later generations have taken: 'A sovereign of suet, a parliament of putty, an aristocracy of alabaster, an intelligentsia of india-rubber, a proletariat of pulp. . . .'.

This last quotation demonstrates Crowley's favourite literary device, and crude though it is, it works quite effectively when he is being indignant or contemptuous. Also when he is characteristically assigning women to their proper place: 'The caresses of no Calypso could chain me in her courts, the cup of no Circe corrupt my chastity, the song of no Siren seduce me to suicide. . . .' (Or, more plainly, 'A man who is strong enough to use women as slaves and playthings is all right'.) Elsewhere the alliterative obsession causes trivialities to assume monstrous proportions—'we hired a hopeless headman, who sub-hired sleepy and sinister servants, and dismissed all these damnable details from our minds'—or else procures a comic effect where none is intended—'I have always had this peculiar passion for putting myself in poisonous perils'—which is characteristic of the striving of the decadents (and alas of Conrad in *Heart of Darkness*) to express the inexpressibly depraved.

There are rather too many anecdotes telling how Crowley strolls casually up some mountain and meets at the top a group of exhausted (though expert) and incredulous climbers who inform him that the route he has just arrived by is notoriously impossible. But it seems that he really was a serious and an intrepid climber. The general reader, with a salt sprinkler to hand, will find this part of his story, along with his travels, the most palatable—and the chapters on Magick the least palatable, if only because human kind cannot bear very much unreality. His estimate of himself as the greatest climber of his time did him little harm, and his view of himself as the greatest English poet of all time probably didn't do much more. But his persuasion that he was a god appears to have had a distinctly deleterious effect on his character as a man.

It was in 1904, in Cairo, that *The Book of the Law* was revealed to Crowley, an event initiating the New Aeon, the third in the history of mankind. The great ethical principle of *The*

Book of the Law is 'Do what thou wilt shall be the whole of the Law', and one of its precepts reads thus: 'Be goodly therefore: dress ye all in fine apparel; eat rich foods and drink sweet wines and wines that foam! Also, take your will and fill of love as ye will, when, where and with whom ye will! But always unto me.' (Crowley glosses the last injunction, in ambiguous fashion, by explaining that the sexual act should always be 'a sacrament'.) He claims to have been shocked by the Law as revealed to him and to have thrust it away from him for as long as he was able, but the cynic may observe that, like many other gospels, it is exactly tailored to its prophet's tastes: for one thing, Crowley was very fond of champagne. Those content with secular explanations of the occult will refer Crowley to his origins, more particularly to his upbringing in an 'Exclusive' Plymouth Brethren household, the extremeness of whose doctrines is illustrated by the fact that Crowley Senior regarded Edmund Gosse's father 'as likely to be damned for latitudinarianism'. Crowley tells us that later in life the caresses of women 'emancipated me from the thraldom of the body' and left his soul 'free to wing its way through endless empyreans and to express its godhead in untrammelled thought of transcendent sublimity. . . .'. At the same time he testifies that 'every woman that I met enabled me to affirm magically that I had defied the tyranny of the Plymouth Brethren and the Evangelicals'.

By his own account women were never in short supply. (And once, womanless in Burma, he had an affair with the resident spirit of a teak tree.) But what is less than endearing is to find Crowley engaged in 'a pageant of purple pleasure and passion' on one page and on very nearly the next denouncing the woman in question as a dipsomaniac or sexual pervert of the squalidest kind. Though he drops a tear when an illegitimately conceived baby of his miscarries, he seems to have been utterly callous in sexual matters—having borrowed some man's wife for a brief whirl, he would return her so readily when called upon ('my cheerful calm daunted them') as to cause more distress and rage in the wife than ever in the husband. 'There is in me Roman virtue,' he tells us, 'and I never shrink from a moral obligation.' Therefore, when he encounters a girl in Russia who 'had passed beyond the region where pleasure had meaning for her', he makes her happy by cheerfully inflicting physical cruelties upon her, justifying his behaviour to the reader on the grounds that, while a small boy would suffer immensely from smoking a cigar, we do not call it cruel to offer a grown man one. Whatever the logic of that, it really doesn't become Crowley to denounce the British for their hypocrisy and then rail at the American nation for its sexual immorality—though I suppose he would answer that the trouble with Americans was that they fornicated for pleasure instead of as 'a sacrament'.

But the sheer arrogance which makes Crowley's confessions initially so readable begins to pall. A revealing story concerns Victor Neuburg, one of his more faithful followers, who later achieved a rather less ambiguous fame as the discoverer of Dylan Thomas, whose early poems he printed in the *Sunday Referee*. This unfortunate young man had fallen in love with a woman called Dorothy—presumptuous of him, since Dorothy was one of the Master's girls!—and Crowley felt he must cure him of his 'romantic idealism'. This he did by allowing Neuburg to become engaged to the girl, and then inviting him to the hotel where the young lover was greeted by the sight of his fiancée, 'unadorned, smoking a cigarette', in Crowley's bed. Later, in Algeria, Crowley decided that Neuburg with 'his shambling gait and erratic gestures' was damaging the Master's prestige in the eyes of the native Mohammedans, so 'I turned the liability into an asset by shaving his head except for two tufts on the temples, which I twisted up into horns. I was thus able to pass him off as a demon that I had tamed and trained to serve me as a familiar spirit. This greatly enhanced my eminence.'

As the book goes on, and Crowley becomes increasingly involved in the occult, so it grows increasingly repellent. There are oases, as when he describes Fifth Avenue as 'a sort of ditch lined with diamonds and over-rouged stenographers, all at a price totally disproportionate to the value of the article', but though the breezy style persists, it is a breeze in a hothouse. While Crowley continues with little self-pity to represent himself as a genius misunderstood, he displays his closest associates as unequivocally squalid or foolish, as weaklings, drunkards, drug addicts, swindlers, pimps, perverts. Yet, like Edmund in *Lear*, Crowley was belov'd—by the faithful Ape of Thoth: or so one would have gathered had not John Symonds told us in his introduction that even she 'found him unbearable after he had become the Ipsissimus'. Magic tends to corrupt, it seems, and absolute magic corrupts absolutely.

Judging from this book, Crowley was a person of astonishing energy and pertinacity, and of remarkable courage, unable to break away from the twin bonds of Plymouthism and Aestheticism; at the best a lesser Wilde, amazing the bourgeoisie at excessive length; at the worst a sinister-shabby megalomaniac, a Nietzsche of the spiritualists. Perhaps the world is fortunate in that he felt nothing but contempt for secular politics. (1969)

INDEX